Red Cape Capers:

Playful Backyard Meditations

Linda Varsell Smith

Thanks to:

Maureen Frank, The Mandala Lady
for preparing the manuscript for printing and designing back cover.

Joanna Rosinska of Primary Remiges
for the front cover and interior artwork.

My poetry friends and family for their support.

ISBN: 978-0-9888554-2-7

Rainbow Communications
4761 NW Hemlock Ave.
Corvallis, OR 97330

www.rainbowcommunications.org

CONTENTS

AUTUMN

WINTER

SPRING

SUMMER

SEASONING

Contemplating in the Backyard

Greeting the sun splaying over the horizon,
leaves on the fruit trees under-lit with light,
I contemplate the dawning of a new day.
Wrapped in a red cape, sitting on a small angel pillow
balanced on my cane/stool, the chi of Gaia
enters my feet to energize my day.

The lawn is parched brown by summer
with green patches of residual spring.
Wormy apples plop to the ground
to be savored and wrapped by my husband,
to last beyond this autumnal season.
Each apple lovingly cut and cored by him
no matter how bruised or penetrated.

Migrating geese and other birds caw in the distance,
some unseen in the canopies of the hazelnut,
cherry, plum and apple trees.
The neighbor's dog barks, fainter barks respond.
No deer, raccoons, nutria detected.
The murmur and whir of nearby traffic
slurs sound and stirs my silence.
Lichen lick the crushed, cracked concrete wall.

As the light shifts, so do my thoughts.
I am new to this morning aubade
designed by a friend to renew my healing.
I am to visualize positive changes,
to connect to what I am to become.

Beads are like rainbows over my watchband.
Time is up for this day.
I fold up the stool, carry pillow and cane into the house.
I hope my cape empowers me like Wonder Woman.

Red Capes

Wrapped in my vibrantly red cape
I step out the back door to the yard
and attempt to connect cosmos and Gaia.
My red cape warms me for contemplation.
Leaves crunch beneath my heavy, black shoes.

Red capes drape Buddhist monks in Bhutan,
enclose a lifetime of spiritual seeking,
begun as young boys.
Monasteries elsewhere host
shorter stays.

I have a red cape and Buddha belly
but the wrong gender and late start.
I can't sit cross-legged on the ground
and rise without assistance even temporarily.
I can't chant their beliefs
or take their spiritual route.
I'll follow different directions,
wear other vestments.

Prayer flags in our fruitful trees
left by a friend years ago
disintegrated in weather.
I miss branches' colorful cotton strips
flowing words with wind
not red flags to spirit,
but quivering rainbow stripes.

Monks spin golden prayer wheels
which ring a bell as they turn.
What delivery system can I conjure
to connect with spirit?
Can I wheel prayers within
and transmit telepathically to angels?
Will I hear bells with my turnings?

Unfurl cape and let me fly from your folds!
I open my red shroud to the sunrise.

Attempting to Meditate

With my Buddha belly
and wearing a red cape
you would think I could reach
a magical, meditative state
in this autumnal garden.

But I am just a fat, old woman
shrouded in her mother's scarlet cape
distracted by the sights and sounds
of this browning backyard.

I sit on a metallic and plastic cane/stool
wearing black, velcro-ed SAS shoes
not barefoot
creating boundaries
to absorbing Gaia's chi.

I am in a pink sweat suit
running from life, surfacing
instead of connecting
to the I AM and Oneness.

I can look for
but not reach
the Prime Life Force.

Angels and guides
strip me divinely naked!

Gardening Details

In dawn-light a solo CD
dangles on a white string
glistening and spinning in the breeze
over an autumnal garden.
A lone red gladiola bloom
does not attract the hummingbird
who hovers over a shriveled blossom.
An earnest small brown bird rustles
in curled, crunchy leaves
pecking the ground.
A stellar jay flits amid the apple branches
accompanied by distant bird-chatter.
Overhead a silent shadow flies East.

Clover clots the lawn.
Weeds choke the garden.
Color cloaked for the season.
Sidewalk chunks build walls
crusty with dried moss,
make plant niches gone to seed.
Gardening tools stack against
green house walls
awaiting an un-constructed shed.

A creature hoots like an owl
who-who   who   who-who   who
who-who   who   who-who   who.
A train whistle stops traffic's mumble
as it rumbles out of sight
signaling this spiritual gardener
to admit meditative defeat
and go inside to begin her day.

Walk With Grounded Light

Whenever you create light, in any situation through your own individual actions, the energy you create changes the energy of Gaia where you walk.
Lee Carroll

Yesterday contrail etches and cloud smudges,
waffles then diffuses in blue sky
over fenced backyard.

Red gladiola adds blooms
trumpets solo surrounded
by withering stalks.

Today fog blurs sunrise
on autumnal equinox
shifting from summer.

Driving to pool for ai chi
car-shine dimmed
my vision obscured.

Fluid movement dances water.
Breathe   think   move
Fog frosts windows.

Next hour sporadic exercise
halts breath, jerks moves
until volleyball with agile crones.

Leaving pool for massage,
sun dissipates most fog. Rhythmic
hands release tightness, oil thought.

She massages sore spots
tenders joints, soothes knots.
I walk out freer.

Loosened limbs
allow liquid movements
to touch earth more steadily.

Driving home - a crumpled box
curled cardboard road kill
litters main drag.

In back yard I sit in lawn chair
ground Gaia's energy
feel gravity on surfaces.
While resting at noonday
lone blooming blood-red gladiola glows
in breeze, catches my breath.

Two bees flit for remnants
of grayish clover buds
ignore radiant leftover dandelion.

Sun-rays penetrate my skin.
I breathe, think, move,
wriggle toes like worms.

Inhale inspiration
exhale co-creations, focus vision
on sun-reddened, closed eyelids.

I stroll to door with spritely step
ready to dance and word-play,
absorbed by lightness.

In a Morning Fog

As I head out the door for my daily
attempt to meditate and commune with nature
in my suburbanized backyard,
I find my husband in headset
listening to NPR as he scurries
about loading his new storage shed.
He places his box of wrapped, wormy apples
in their niche as carefully and agilely as a squirrel,
rattles ladders about, clinks and clanks tools,
sweeps dirt from the stone foundation
into gathering fog.
He said at six he could see stars and the moon
but as sun rose, fog rolled in.

I should have delayed until 8
this rendezvous with Gaia,
to read the newspapers and accompany
my pills with low-fat, blueberry yogurt.
It is Saturday and I have time for lollygagging
rather than dash to the pool first.

How can I quiet my mind now
with my husband hustling about,
while I sit cradled in a camp chair.
I am applauding the good news::
a six century old Chinese tradition
of a three-day dog eating festival has ended,
due to tens of thousands of protests
lead by Internet netizens
in behalf of thousands of slaughtered dogs.

Locally our artists display their wares
at the Fall Festival in Central Park.
It is supposed to be sunny by this afternoon
when the college's football team game begins.
No more flyovers and cannon blasts from stadium
which disturbed local dogs and community citizens.

But I must concentrate on now.
A blue jay swipes a hazelnut overhead,
plops it a few feet from me
and flies to an adjacent apple tree.
The jay then drops to the lawn
to snatch the hazelnut,
flies to another apple tree
to savor the find.
Then jay chirps to feathered friends
to come and chomps on some filberts.

Each day I try to sit at a different spot
to envision a different view.
I have tried to steer clear of apple trees
as the yard is littered with fallen fruit.
An apple could bop me.

Morning sounds of bird chirps
and traffic whirrs distract me.
Today I notice a reddening tree
in the back neighbor's yard.
I do not know them.

My thoughts race to plans for the day.
I fold up my chair and hand it
to my husband to store in the shed.
It is supposed to rain tomorrow.
I will try again to connect with nature
seated on a dry chair under an umbrella.
I'll read newspapers and eat after coming outside.
Maybe I'll beat the rain and greet the sun.

Cover-ups in Cloudy Light

Gray clouds roll in portending predicted rain.
In un-shrouded intensity, sun
plays peek-a-boo with rushing clouds,
radiates then darkles.

I head for our newly-build backyard shed
where I store a blue camp chair.
I retrieve the folded chair stalked against beige wall
amid lawn gear and boxed wrapped apples.
Whiffs of new plastic waft to brisk breeze.

Planting the open chair
I prepare to absorb Gaia's energy–
chi through the feet
stardust from the cosmos.

Plunked, scaly, windfall apples
cluster around the chair.
I adjust my red cape
over my exposed knees.
Short nightgown crumbles
angel and stars print.

Last surviving red gladiola bloom
remains hidden from view
behind cherry tree trunk.
A lone bee scurries nearby,
rustles in grass and fallen leaves
then flies away.

Facing in-and-out sun,
hunkered behind clouds,
rays emerge to glow in cloud flow.
Sun perched above neighbor's roof line
flickers like strobe-light enlightenment.

A massive gray cloud passes.
A pocket of sunshine radiates through,
but I am chilled as breezes sneak
under my cape, behind my bent knees.

I head inside to warm,
hope my feet absorbed some chi.
As cosmic light obscures,
my vision shutters.
Juggling water bottle and open chair
I stumble toward the shed,
cape blowing in breeze.

Chair folds up and leans against wall.
Door closes without lock or key.
My conjurer's cape cloaks my covert operations
for connection on this clouding day.

After the Rain Returns

Long-delayed rain has arrived.
It is more fun to meditate in the backyard
when it is warmer and sunnier.

I'd better not sit under a tree.
Heavier winds might plop raindrops on me
even after the storm has passed.

Branches on peach, pear, cherry,
apple and hazelnut trees have sprouted green fuzz
beside the gray-green crusty scabs.

Rain polka-dotted a three-leaf clover
and spotted blades of grass
to glisten, even in muted light.

Our summer-tanned lawn increases its green factor.
Leaf-curls nestle, dried-out grass revives.
Weeds thrive in the garden.

Unnecessary, coiled green hose
curls on concrete. Nozzle—
the head of a slumbering snake.

Newly-built storage shed
has not been loaded with white plastic buckets,
gardening tools and crumpled small pool.

Noise from my neighbor's chainsaw
disturbs any attempts at concentration.
My attention is drawn outward.

I am having more fun
observing what is outside of me
than contemplating what is latent within me.

Barking Up the Wrong Tree

My acupuncturist suggests
I could conduce wood energy
if I put my barefoot against
the bark of a tree trunk.
She demonstrates placing
her bare foot against the smooth-sided
white massage table leg.
Similarly, in the pool
I stretch my calves against
concrete pool side in swim shoes,

I would try this against bark, but
I am diabetic. I should not
go barefoot and risk foot injury.
She says leather soles best, but
the soles of my shoes are rubber
which insulates me from lightning strikes
and from absorbing Gaia's chi.

Surveying the most accessible trees
I discover bark has different patterns.
Some have more loped limbs, knots and whorls.
Cherry bark rings horizontally
with oval dots running like Morse Code.
Filbert's trunk ripples smoothly to the ground,
river-teeth of moss and lichen patches.
Apple bark is scaly, vertical rivulets
cushioned by moss at the base.
Does moss create a barrier or soft cushioning?
The towering evergreen is much too rough
for stocking feet–a scratchy conduit.
Besides rain lingers on the grass
to dampen my heels. No sap in these socks.

She says the idea may be a little woo-woo anyway.
I spot the mossy sidewalk chunks
creating garden walls.
What about rock energy?
On a sunny day the rocky mini-plateaus
could warm and twitch toes,
prance and dance my feet.
I could greet sunrise in hole-ly socks
extending my arms to cosmic rays
or be a lazy dog lifting leg toward tree
and not touching.

Serotinal

Dust motes float
shine in window light.
I breathe aerial sparkles.

Pillow-propped on the bed
I watch dust dance
dart in and out of light.

Labor Day weekend ends.
Schools begin.
Blankets return.

Most of the fruit harvested.
Filberts gone.
Flowers bloom last hurrahs.

Picnic orts on grass
crumbs of summer
before bite of fall.

I place feet on the floor.
try to lighten
tiptoe into autumn.

Tweaking Space

> *Women are looking for meaning. What is missing from their lives is that inner place of heart, soul and wisdom where few of us spend much time. We're too busy to create a place of quietude- unplugged rather than unhinged.* Kathleen Parker

Women get their best creative ideas in the shower.
Away from it all.....apparently.
So why am I soul-searching sitting in the backyard
hoping some of Gaia's chi will rev me up?

Backyard background noises can be distracting
but a shower does not seem a better alternative
as a place to muse and meditate.
I do not want to be unplugged, but to plug in.

This poetry-wonk will be a fair-weather backyard friend.
I will don a red cape when ambiance chills,
and doesn't tend to induce warm thoughts on the cosmos.
which seems indifferent to our presence.

Sitting in front of a lighted computer,
or during TV ads can be fallow time,
or waiting for appointments with a magazine
or a notebook for quotes you notice when reading.

I try to take a nap to calm hyper-mind,
doze from a snoozer-book.
Could try shamanistic techniques
to transport to a deeper or lighter place.

Creative sparks arrive when awake or asleep
provide insights to probe further.
Open or close eyes to surprises.
I may never be fully wise, soulful, heart-filled—
     but I'll be creatively searching new spaces.

Emigrants

As I walk to the backyard today
I pick up my camp chair–not put away.

Perhaps seeds think the blue seat is sky
and migrated here to settle, supply?

Maple samaras on patio —our neighbors' seed?
Who sends flighty immigrants we don't need?

Other seeds turn beige on patio pavers.
Some stay on stone, while movers are savers.

Some dandelion and buttercup migrants–mowed.
Don't know from where they were sowed.

I escaped seasonal fruit flies bugging me inside
and joined insect emigrants around me outside.

Yesterday we sprayed settled carpenter ants.
Some undercover migrants don't get a chance.

My red cape was passed on to me —my mother's
now on another plane, beloved by many others.

We are all emigrants in time and place
seeking a nourishing, special space.

A friend said from eleven to one
are best vitamin D rays from the sun.

Gusty winds bring rain, it's time to go.
I carry chair and myself toward the patio.

Deer Visitor

At first the doe rests on a nest of leaves
amid the fruitless backyard.
She is alone. Sometimes bucks
walk down the suburban street
into our yard to graze and sleep.

After a few hours she stands, grooms
and nibbles red leaves beside the fence.
We do not have much to eat.
Fruit and nuts are gone.
She is thin, but without warts.

My grandson and I peer at her
through the rain-smudged window.
She sees us and looks away undaunted.
We take her picture in various poses.
She's shielded by glass and wall.

We move away to other tasks
and when we check on her, she's left.
It is near noon when she goes to find
more abundant pastures and company.
Another traveler doing the best she can.

Oh Dear Deer!

This morning the doe slept
in a bed of leaves.

Later she stood and groomed
before nibbling leaves.

Now it is getting dark
and she's still here.

She faces west
ears perked.

Many deer pass through
but usually briefly.

Hidden in brown by day.
Blotted by night.

Deer in Autumn

camouflaged by fallen leaves
beside a weathered wooden fence
a doe rests in a nest of browned leaves

statue-still she is barely seen
until she stands to nibble red leaves
against the fading fence

barren fruit and nut trees
dangle remnant leaves
scrawl scowling sky

her ears twitch, seek sound.
she detects our movements
but remains steadfast

Nearing Thanksgiving

Leaves from fruit and nut trees
float down and pile on mounding ground.
Sun makes browning leaves more golden.

I watch from a washed window.
Another family emergency keeps
my ear toward coiling-cord phone.

Watching withering leaves falling
like my stiffened spirits and haunted heart,
I seek hibernation.

My thoughts chill and toss
like airborne leaves
out of control.   Hope dying.

Pointillist painting on lawn,
swishes of wishes
will blow away in the first wind.

What will I be thankful for
in two weeks and who
will be with me?

Poinsettia Sprig Before Thanksgiving

A sprig of poinsettia
remained outside in a grocery cart,
spread like an opened heart
on the portion for small items or purse.

In frosty fog
on black plastic cart flap
red petals splay with green leaves
with stray spray of red.

I put the sprig in another cart
to brighten someone else
and went inside to shop.
When I came out it was still there.

A man began cramming carts
to move a long row.
The poinsettia was about to be crushed.
I grabbed the burst of red.

At home the piece of poinsettia
dwells in a blue glass
in lukewarm water
and longs for the rest of the plant.

Perhaps the crinkles will ease.
From the counter to dining table
the sprig is the center of attention
until it withers before Thanksgiving.

Windfall

Apples drop in heated breeze
some carry scales and worms.
Deer and people pick them up,
devour them sliced, diced or whole.

In kitchen sink pesticide-free
apples bobble, jammed tight
for storage in refrigerator
or wrapped in newspaper in shed.

My husband carves out each blemish
and savors each morsel.
I have not watched deer dining manners.
A friend gathers them for her horse.

I prefer apple sauce or apple pie.
As they polka-dot the lawn,
ripe and delicious, I ponder if
I should harvest some....not happening.

Trying to Do

*Meditate: To think contemplatively, muse, reflect. To intend to do or
achieve: plan.* - Random House College Dictionary

With the mantra "Don't try, just do"
marching my morning thoughts,
I trudge to the backyard to meditate
seeking sun on the horizon.
My mother said, "If something's worth doing,
it's worth doing well."

Somehow I recall you need
to quiet and empty your mind
to meditate properly.
My buzzing brain and poetic leaps
make the concept daunting.

But you do what you think you have to do,
so I head to the shed to retrieve my blue camp chair,
plant it on uneven ground,
wrap my red cape snug to cover
bare legs dangling from angels and stars
cotton patterned nightgown
and shiver in the autumn chill.

Unbrushed teeth chatter in the cold.
Mobile phone in chair awaits
return call to confirm whether
my dental cleaning is at 8 as my husband
jotted from a reminder call yesterday
or at 1 which has been on my calendar for months.

My thoughts drift to Kip, my celestial son
a dashing flash of light, an eternal flame
on his spiritual journey across the cosmos.
I have tried to release tying him to the Earth
with my tugging grief, so he can fulfill his destiny.
I do miss him, but do not want
to impede his lofty ascent.

Thoughts ground to earthbound
children and grandchildren
and what challenges they face
on this incarnation's trip.

The solo red gladiola bloom remains closed.
Will it open this chilling day
with muted sun?

Birds cackle, "You have as much chance
trying to meditate as you do losing weight."
I'll wing-it my own way.

My red cape will cocoon creativity.
I will open my cloak to butterfly poems.
But now I will go inside to warm up.

My pillbox is unfilled.
I refill pills, nibbling low-fat yogurt.
I find three prescriptions
will not make it through the week.
Three times I flub automatic ordering
by touch dial up.
Such tiny numbers on the containers!
Hard to transfer digits to the phone.

At least my eye appointment
is a written mailed reminder
on the counter to calendar
for next week.
My vision should clear.

The confirmation dentist's call for 1
came too late to go to the pool at 8.
But tomorrow I will greet sunrise
with a smile gleaming toward light.

Dampened Spirits

Moistened after two hours in the pool
I carry a blue camp chair
into the dimmed backyard.

I am still wet behind the ears
in my attempt to meditate,
so I will contemplate what appears.

Gray clouds crowd.
Grass still damp from early morning rain.
My red cape cocoons from chill.

Each morning I position the chair
in a different spot
for shifting viewpoints.

Solo gladiola blasts its last bloom.
Remnant rose blushes blanched tips.
Closed dandelion-dot snakes toward me like a cobra.

Garden devas must appreciate rain's assist
after weeks of sun-cracking clay,
roots seeking water, blooms beaming toward light.

Distant din of birdcalls,
drone of traffic–
unseen sound lulls me.

Plucked from chair pocket,
water bottle re-hydrates me.
I relax and rest my eyes.

When I open my eyes
through a gap of bush hedge, a peephole
to spy splash of purple blooms next door.

Chilled, dampened
I lug the chair across the lawn
to leave in the storage shed.

Gray hovers. Heavy air.
How I thirst for color,
to breathe dry heat.

Dawning Light

Orange sunrise splays rays
between open spaces
of bushes in backyard hedge.

Neighbor's wooden fence
stakes a boundary
nearer our houses.

But our backyards butt
garden to garden
in orderly harmony.

Weeds remain a chaotic remnant
in the harvested areas–
wildly, flagrantly errant.

I am a weed
as yellowing rays tamp
the butch-cut lawn.

Emanations

Every artifact, every natural object, with its ghostly wrappings or associations and meanings, begotten and forgotten, is a gathering of minds or contending voices, every thing is an invisible assembly. Robert Pinsky

My red cape contends with my quagmire of quarks.
Hovering cape connects me
with shriveled red remnant gladiola
bent bloom sheath arcing in autumnal air.

Leaves curl and cover lawn reviving with rain
from arid summer, layering for winter.
Windfall apples collected and wrapped in newspaper
with their worms, scales, bruises–packed away.

Recent neighbor pounds replacement slats in our back fence,
recalls former neighbors who lived in that house.
We knew them better
and repaired the wood fence together.

All the particles swirling in the moist wind,
arriving in mizzle churn, combine sparks of life.
Auras, shades, ghostly palimpsests from other dimensions
determined star dust descendants create our destinies,

So much unknown, unseen, untouched, unheard.
So much begotten we have forgotten. Clutch what you can.
Backyard thoughts drift up front in my mind.
Warm elusive memories swarm as I hug cape snug.

Revenant

Fall's grayed sky relapses
into a sunny, summery day
lightening the backyard.

In childhood I conjured fairies
flitting and scrambling in trees and bushes
instead of jays and squirrels.

Garden's blooms and holes held shelter for elves,
the castles in the sandbox terra-formed
into a whimsical landscape.

This shriveling garden's harvest is gone.
Leaf-cradles rock on withered flowerbed.
Stalks droop, not strut.

When I approach the back door,
it had locked behind me. I walk around the house
to find the front door locked.

Before I fumble for hidden key, I see red holly berries.
How I wish I could see fairies nibbling them!
My inner child yearns to open the door.

Overcasting

On an overcast October morning
I sit on my blue camp chair
hands tucked under my red cape.

New wood or repaired slats
glare beside weathered gray fence
draw my attention to lighter places.

Buds no longer bloom.
Fewer windfall apples.
Leaves raked.

Only lavender puffs of clover
amid chunks of sidewalk wall.
No berries on the vines.

I overcast stitches of light
over my gloomy hem of grief—
mend, heal.

Warm hands on lap,
no longer sewing,
I free myself for prayer.

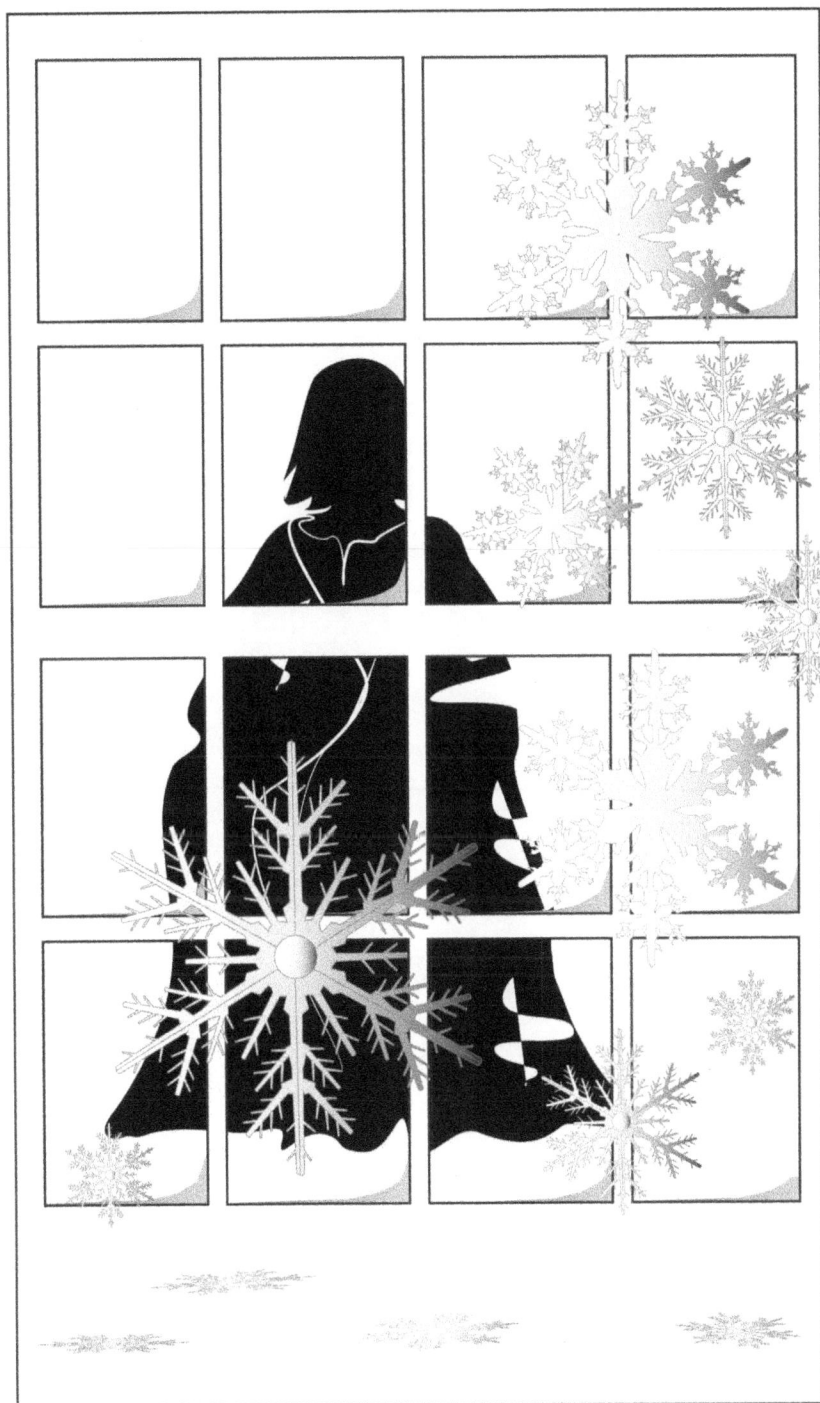

Aubade

Let us cultivate our gardens. Voltaire

Recent sunrise aids finding newspapers
strewn on driveway and stuffed in nook near mailbox–
both papers covered with plastic bags
to recycle to dog lovers' use.
Swim shoe slippers flap on concrete.

The house is silent except for tick of clock,
whoosh of heat and rustle of pages.
After morning rituals, the day usually begins
with the solace of warm water ai chi in the pool.
But today I will attend a talk on Candide
at continued learning.

Awakening too early
after wrestling for hours
with a family issue,
this morning is quiet only outside
not inside me
where I am digging deep.

When Weeds Wheeze

Sunrise blushes behind cloud-fans,
fades to blue.

Weeds gasp last pollen, before first frost,
face wind extinction.

Arthritis inflames aches,
movement slows in fall's chill.

Leaf shadows on tree trunks shift.
Trees stretch shadows across the lawn.

My standing shadow darkens grass.
I stare at the remaining apples–clinging.

God Helmet

If I am to meditate in the backyard
maybe I should get a God Helmet.
Scientists say they can create
a spiritual experience with a wired
helmet to stimulate a special spot in the brain
with electromagnetic waves.

This helmet looks like a football helmet.
which didn't protect some players' brains.
How would this helmet scramble mine?
Maybe the God Helmet is mind control
like a Japanese death cult who wore wired helmets
before sabotaging subway with sarin.

Apparently we have a God gene
to predispose us to believe
in the supernatural.
Some claim aliens tampered
with our DNA long ago
and we are still under their control.

Cult leaders, killers, visionaries, druggies,
mediums, shaman, psychics, alien abductees
reach other states of consciousness
and claim contact with alternate dimensions.
Others with under-activated God genes
stuck to earthly 3-D realm, cannot see.

How much control of our genes do we have?
Lots of genetic testing and research going on.
How do we connect or disconnect God?
I'll put on my red cape and tie-dye cap
to protect me from the sun and rogue rays,
knowing reality may be an illusion like a God Particle.

Show and Tell

When people show you what they are– believe them. Maya Angelou

What do the backyard creatures and features think of us?
Does rock wall realize it is recycled sidewalk chunks?
Does wooden fence resent not being painted?
Do fruit trees know they have not been sprayed?
Do weeds appreciate they have not been yanked?
Do flowers enjoy not being picked?
Do berry and veggie garden patches feel neglected?
Do patio pavers covet the protective moss?
Does backyard greet all aerial orts with enthusiasm?

We don't dig for worms for fish bait.
Birds devour our cherries without much contest.
Bugs of all sorts have mostly free reign.
Seeds are flung flagrantly. Cats deposit openly.
Scales form on the apples unscathed.
Compost heap teems mostly untended.
Storage shed await tools and plastic pool.
Ladder leans mostly undisturbed on sidewall.
Camp chair languishes moist and sun-faded.
They depend on weather's mercy.

Do they want any of our interventions?
We are pretty much live-and-let-live in the backyard–
rather laissez-faire with our supposedly less sentient neighbors.
It's not always the same way with people.
People resent other people's interventions,
make their judgments and act according to will.
They show and tell us their intentions.
Belief comes hard with beloveds
when they show characters that break our heart.
The backyard displays its own nature and a bit of ours.

Snowbound

A freak winter storm covers our yard in snow.
Icicles drip from the roof.
Branches rime.
Holly berries peek under white caps.
An unfamiliar landscape conceals colors.
Immobilized objects snuggle in snow.

Elsewhere, the Martian rover Curiosity
uncovers signs of an ancient freshwater lake
with earth-like chemistry and nutrients
near their equator, perhaps once
a watering hole for life before drying up.
Mars does have polar snow.

Elsewhere, puzzled scientists find HD 106906b
a massive planet eleven times bigger than Jupiter
that does not follow rules for planet or sun formation.
60 billion miles away it is the first of its kind found.
Planets, close to young stars form from gas,
dust, asteroid-like debris.   Any snow somewhere?

Warm inside my house with most holiday decorations
completed, but few presents bought,
I think of all the billions of planets in multiverses
and wonder if other beings are delighted
and inconvenienced by snowy, fluffy stuff,
or other dazzling droplets from the sky.

Snow Storm #2

snow-stressed evergreens
snow-clumped and drooped holly
limp, wimpy people

holly berries lure.
bird-bends on snowy branches
trickle mini-snow-drifts

robins quiver branches
bounce berries   drip snow
fly to other limbs

holly berries like blood drops
from pricked red-breasted birds
branch red respite

icicles drip sunlight
snow plowed pile shrinks
snow-folks slump

rime melts from branches
fog hovers over snow
pathways clear

Frost Quakes

As the Midwest experiences frost quakes,
the Northwest is in the midst of its second snow storm.
Here the plows are on alert.
City and county road crews coordinate efforts
to deal with snow and freezing rain.
No de-icing, but an anti-icing agent
on bridges and shaded curves.
Critics hope the city handles
this second storm better than the first.

Our town shut down. Schools closed.
Transit systems avoid hills.
Snow covers sound. All is quiet,
      unlike the Midwest when the Super Bowl fans'
      noise competed with Midwest frost quakes'
      creaks, crackles and pops, rumbling,
      sounds like snowballs thrown against houses,
      strange unknown noises and flashes of light.
      Temperatures in both arenas were frigid.
      Seahawks credit the booming 12th man for victory.

Cryoseism caused by abrupt temperature swings
and ground moisture freezing and expanding,
are not detected by seismograph
because they are near the surface. But frost quakes
move ground and rock, generate sound waves,
crack foundations, damage water and natural gas lines.
      Whereas, our snowstorm muffles sound
      and just knocks vehicles off course.
      Perhaps a power failure, burst pipes,
      but many are prepared for these infrequent events.
      Today men braved snowfall to put a moisture barrier
      under our house to protect our walls and floors.

With climate changes, everyone has to adapt
to weird weather and adopt new coping strategies,
examine priorities and predict heart-weather.
Perhaps there will be thawing of cold heart-charts,
but right now the snowflakes layer like icing.

Dream Catcher

The young man cleaning the tables
in McDonalds liked my blue sweat shirt.
with three wolves around a dream catcher
under a full white and blue-tinged moon.
The phrase below says:
Nothing can hold back a dream.
The sweat shirt is from Lillooet, B.C. Canada.

He said he was from the Wolf Clan
and showed me his forearm with a colorful tattoo
of a dream catcher with a black wolf paw in the circle.
He said the tattoo artist combined
three designs to create it.
He was very proud of the outcome..
The tattoo was easily seen
below his short-sleeved black uniform.

He left his family in 2001 for Oregon
and had not been back but once
on a sad occasion for the funeral
of his cousin. He did not say
why he went away.

As he swished the tables
he did not tell me the dreams
imbedded in his arms.

Sugar Time

What is left? Loss remains lost.
There is enough accumulated in my life
to know we do not get over
piles of crushed sugar under our pillows.
                                Kirsten Rian

I can only dream of sugar lumps
clumped inside my pillow
chunks of sweetness
covered with puffy white feathers
perhaps fallen from angel wings
to lift my spirits.
My enclosed pillows rest on flattened sheets.

Crushed sugar runs in my veins.
Bloodied goodness
excreted from my body
but not my brain.
Loss remains lost,
but what is left
is lingering longing
billowing pillows
for what is sweet, good
energizing hope.

Between Extremes
Think higher. Feel deeper. Elie Wiesel

A puddle in patio's blue camp chair seat
keeps me inside viewing dampened backyard.
Sun symbols on the side wall.
Rain-battened aerial-lint of buzz and fuzz.
Sky-fabric thick, moist and gray.

Vision smudged and snug in red cape I gaze.
Cleansed air brushes branches.
Few raindrops drip from the roof,
don't drool down windowpanes.
Soggy flowers flop.

I struggle for lofty thoughts
with a cotton ball taped to my writing arm
like a bug bite gone rogue
after a multi-vial blood draw.
Thankfully a hole-in-one.

Drained after seesaw
of anxiety and elation
with doctor and relationships
I am unbalanced, incapable of depth—
lulled between storms.

Gray sky weighs on me.
Green slate floor does not cushion cold
like grasping grass protects roots.
If I lubricate with hot green tea
will warmth flow within me?

Heights and depths out of reach
inside or outside of me.
I am between extremes
in limbo on this plane
yearning to root or branch.

Inside Meditation

Inside an enclosed room
called the Moon Room
with a recently renovated roof
room contents not fully put in place,
I look toward the backyard,
wear a red cape flowing like petals,
write at a picnic table
sit on a creaky Hitchcock chair
with a blue cushion.

Overcast sky dulls the lavish
red, pink and purple
azaleas and rhododendrons,
scraggly, needs-to-be-mowed lawn,
hidden patches for raspberries,
strawberries, blueberries,
leafy apple, hazelnut, cherry, peach, pear, plum—
trees without fruit and nuts .

I look at sun symbols on the gray-green wall,
feet on cold, green slate floor
and yearn the return of sun and warmth
to meditate outside amid blooming spring.

My Nose Job
When you can't hide it, flaunt it.

When the dermatologist declared
the pimple on my nose a carcinoma—
slow growing but in need of removal,
I was shocked that a foggy Oregonian,
not a sun-worshipper should have this condition.

I was assured it could be from childhood
sun exposure tinily tunneling my nose.
I recalled some teenage beach burnings
where I broiled in oils, reddened and pealed.
Then there were the graduate school years
in Arizona, no sun screen but sunglasses.
Occasional trips to the Southwest and California
relied on a hat for coverage.

Most recently my fair weather meditations
in the backyard, faced unfiltered sun,
baking mostly covered except
for my unprotected face. No make-up
to block sun-rays. I rarely wear even lipstick.

As I become a crone, I have noticed
age spots, moles, dry skin and various
barnacles of aging as a friend says. But
I did not notice the cancer cells.

When another doctor used the MOHL
method to remove the cell cluster,
he numbed my nose and gouged it out.
I saw the red dot amid the pinky-gray tissue.
He claims he got it all.

I am to keep my nose higher than my heart.
Take it easy a few days.
My nose job will make my nose thinner.
My nose must not be exposed to air.
Daub Vaseline to prevent scabs and scars
and apply a consistent bandage.
The first white bandage created
a humongous honker. But soon
a boring beige Band Aid arced
over the absorbable stitches.

Today I put on a colorful patterned bandage
as I heal my wounded nose.
The bandage has red bows on a blue background.
which matches my blue outfit and rainbow eye-lace.
When I am able to stick my nose
into heartbreaking issues, I hope
there is a bandage for my heart.

Today I bend to retrieve Valentine's Day
decorations containing heart-filling creatures
from the bottom of my closet.
My nose-dive lifts my spirits.
and enhances heart-felt healing.

Rainbows in the Clouds

Today we celebrate Martin Luther King Jr.
who lead civil rights struggles for equal justice.
We still march and protest for enlightenment.

Maya Angelou believes we should bring light
into our life and the lives of others.
We should be rainbows in the clouds.

As I survey the fogged-in winter landscape,
moist and gray like a cloud,
rainbows will stay metaphoric here.

Rain-fed moss on tree trunks,
lush lawn, but no flowers in the garden.
Beige filbert filaments dangle like bracelets.

Through the window muted colors
await sun as I sit still, silent and dry,
waiting to be inspired.

Yesterday, before sunset, the cast of Selma marched
from Selma City Hall to over Edmund Pettus bridge
singing the song "Glory", cresting at the top of the bridge.

Oprah Winfrey said they were remembering
Martin Luther King as an idea of what can happen
with strategy, discipline and love.

This week is a week of service
and commemoration of what is possible
and what still needs to be done.

What will I do to bring rainbows,
penetrate the fog to create bridges of light,
when surrounded by so many clouds?

Something is Everywhere

Our life goes on in every instant in every word. Tadeusz Dabrowski

From nano, micro places
to macro, infinite spaces
organized and energized
by codes like DNA , gravity
or electro-magnetism– in many forms
from many materials– whatever the sizes
something is everywhere.

Mysterious dark matter,
a particle zoo,
to perceived sentient creatures
we encounter this life
on this planet.
and speculate existence elsewhere—
there is nothing nowhere.

It is a miracle we are not crushed
by such abundance of matter
not zapped by all the communication waves,
or choked by strained polluted air from the ages.
These fragile, often diseased bodies
with limited sensory skills
still try to understand it all.

Our words shared by sound
or written, buzz in our brains.
Even in our sleep, life goes on.
In every instant
conscious creations
here and in hidden dimensions
speak to the grandeur of ALL.

Contemplating Spring Garden Meditations

After turbulent winter, during April's rain respites,
I will return to renewing, calming meditations in the garden;
don my red cape;
wear my tie-dye cap,
carry a camp chair,
bring a diet beverage,
and a notepad and pen,
to create a poem-a-day
for National Poetry Month;
draw Gaia's chi
through the soles of my SAS black, velcro shoes
to meditate on observations and connections,
try not to get distracted by roofers, painters,
renovation detritus; lawn mowing,
flamboyant red rhododendrons,
try to focus on some colorful spot or idea,
bring balance, insight, creativity and harmony
to my meandering mind;
however I remember fall meditations,
paying attention to what was outside
not inside of me,
until it became too cold
to cocoon in my cape,
unable to avoid shivering
and quivering hands
before hibernating until spring—
warmth and sun's renewal;
still my cape makes sure
I am warm enough to heat my heart and core,
but I will not greet the sun at dawn like in the fall,
I will sleep in, assess the weather
perhaps do some indoor meditations
facing the garden, gazing through the window,
comfortably at a table (with bouquet) to write on,
sucking-up Gaia's chi
through a green slate floor mimicking grass,
seeking sun's rays in a windless, dry room
shrouded in my red cape.

Backyard Spring Images

amid apple memories anticipating windfalls
    azaleas now pink and red blooms emblazon fences

bulbs, buds, blooms, bugs, birds, blueberries, bushes, balls
    each have their seasonal hurrah

camping chairs for meditating and chatting
    with family and friends rotating crops
        compost pile marinates before recycling

deer, some with viral warts, sleep under trees
    detritus from recent roofers and renovators remain

evergreens oversee Easter Egg Hunts
    eager children scavenge for plastic, money-filled eggs

flowers on their floral time-tables petal on schedule
    fence weathers, wooden replaced stats lighter
        fascia's dry-rotted replacements require painting

gutters on roof re-connected, some on ground
    gardens of berries, vegetables now in process

hazelnut tree faces nibblers when nuts arrive
    house- green and gray reflect Oregon's greening and fog

insects arrive, migrate inside
    inrush of ideas when contemplating creations

jabberwocky from my mind and pen when I sit in backyard
    jets make contrails   jays chew cherries

keeping order of chaotic growth is husband's job.
    kindling from pruned branches seek fireplaces

ladder rests against overhang, waits for lollygagging painters
    lawn has various cuts, butch-cut to hippie

mowing the lawn   maintenance of gardens
        meditation when seasonally sensible
                might consider spring a good time to begin

noise from planes, birds, machines,
        roofers' hip-hop music disturbs calm
                headset used when husband outside working
                        neighbors beyond fence rarely see each other

orchard of fruit and nut trees
        seasonal changes bring pickers and peckers

pear, plum, peach trees join apple and cherry abundance
        plants in transition seed to weed   sustenance or beauty

quagmire of squishy, mushy mud
        when overcome with rain

roofers and renovators leave reflective roof and sun tunnel
        rhododendrons now attract attention
                raspberries soon on stage

seeds thrust, strawberries maturing
        storage shed empties and fills
                sidewalk-chunk walls grow moss

traffic noise muffled by trees
        Tilapia pond memories,
                birds plucked goldfish and water leaks

underground and understory churning
        uncorked yard work projects emerging

variety of vegetables
        variable depending on intentions
                and actual planting, dormant this moment

worms wriggle   windows wait for water
     watering vegetation with hoses and rain
         walls create boundaries and steps

xeriscape endures many attempts to capture water
     tried trapping roof water through tube and underground to pond
         ditches drain and divert water

yarn remnants which held shiny CD's to detour birds
     dangle from branches in the yard

zzz   napping on a lounger or blanket

Burgeoning Spring

Cataracts ripen, blur details and color
hobbled knees seek blue camp chair
unfolding like petals
I sit on red cape bundled into a cushion,
wear tie-dye cap to protect balding spot.
In one chair pocket is blueberry green tea
in a cobalt glass.
Warm hands grab pen
open blank paged notebook
to record any insights or observations

Breathing deeply hands on thighs
palms facing upward toward sun
I see an aqua wading pool lapping like a tongue
over stacked wood and plastic pails.
A ladder hangs on outside wall.
Fruit-less and nut-less trees engulfed in leaves
cast shifting shadows on grass
beside angular shadows
of three gables and the storage shed.
A dried Christmas wreath leans against an evergreen
still with fading red bow.
Two dandelions pop yellow.
Bugs buzz fly-by.
Whangdoodles would be welcome.

Thoughts flit from aging ailments, backyard images
to the cosmos and basic origins of existence.
What is illusion and what is real?
Why and how was this universe created?
Our sun expands to sterilize us.
Hits from asteroids and gamma rays could incinerate Earth.
Galaxies dance and collide.
Atoms re-organize, re-configure.
Dark matter and gravity battle
to Big Crunch or Big Chill—
or something else.

Human survival in space travel?
Transverse universes? Dimensional transfers?
Technological advances?
But are we worth saving?
Will our end come from lack of stewardship
and human miscalculations?

My closed eyes conjure red-rim around
a green amoeba shape on eye lids.
Sun soothes my limbs.
Back to sun shades face.
Does Gaia's chi penetrate shoes,
snake up aluminum chair frame
across fabric like space/time?

Dressed in black sweat pants
Hazel Hall black tee-shirt
with her black and white image
and her red words—:
I am blinded by the space between me and the inevitable.

Spring Sapling

The lone leaf clinging all winter
fell in a recent storm.
A rusted pipe with beige cord
reach out two arms
to tether the sapling upright,
support spring budding.

At the base, black mulch mounds
surrounded by rain-lush grass.
A blue plastic tag dangles
from a spindly branch
a loose bracelet
fades in sporadic sun.

Green moss pimples the bark
on this adolescent trunk
struggling for growth.
Today a gentle rain tamps
up-reaching, gangly limbs.

First Food Feast at Celilo Village

Dancing, drumming and celebrating
the springtime bounty,
tribal belief is the salmon arrival
fulfills its promise to return after winter subsides.
But there were not many salmon for feasting,
since nontribal sports and commercial
anglers caught thousands of chinook
including from Bonneville's spawning grounds.

The Yakima Nations ceremonial fishermen
caught 21 spring chinook setting nets
for six days and five nights near the village
to feed about 800 people.
The Warm Springs tribes sent 50 more
chinook caught at Cascade Locks
and 40 frozen from last year.

In the long houses the feasts are annual reminders
of the loss of salmon runs,
the damming of Celilo Falls with Dallas Dam.
The nontribal fishers fish seven days a week.
They are supposed to share the catch.
Wild salmon are under The Endangered Species Act.
They suffered from construction of upriver dams
and overfishing despite quotas.

The salmon and the tribes struggle to survive
as the state collects revenue from fishing licenses.
Tribal fishermen barely have enough salmon
for their ceremonies.

The feast tradition comes from The Seven Drums
or Washat religion of the plateau tribes.
When the Creator prepared to bring people to Earth
a council of plants and animals convened
to ask for gifts for the new creatures.
Salmon offered its body for food.
Water, deer, roots and berries were other first foods.
The ceremonies include all these first foods.

No one can see the salmon before it is brought out to cook.
Sorrowful or angry emotions must not be passed on to eaters.
Tribal members could go downstream to catch early fish
but tradition says the salmon must return
to traditional fishing areas and long houses.
The tribes have fishing rights by treaty.
They want less intense fishing below Bonneville
in the early season. Idaho upstream is also a problem.
All fishermen long for the spring chinook season,
waiting since the previous fall.
The mists and roar of Celilo Falls
from the fishing scaffolds,
destroyed in 1957
remain haunting memories of abundance.

St. Patrick's Day

Much of the country
blanched by snow
but Oregon is green.

The lawns need mowing
between rains.
Buds burst technicolor..

Holly berries plucked
leaving the branches
prickly green.

As Irish celebrate
our grandson with a smidgen of Irish
visits from kiwi New Zealand.

Yesterday the family gathered
to love-welcome him home
with shamrocks, leprechauns.

Spring means beginnings for us all.
Greening becomes blooming
hopefully with Irish luck.

Rang Barse Holi Festival of Colors

Its just-turned spring and color flings.
The Hindu Festival for the triumph
of good defeats evil is here

Holika, a demon was a sister
of Hiranyahkashya, a demon king
who considered himself
ruler of the universe,
but he had a son Prahalad
who followed Vishnu.

The king wanted to kill
his disloyal son, but Vishnu
saved him from burning.
When Holika, who was immune to fire
tried to help her brother,
she turned to ashes because
she used her powers for evil.

The fable lead to Holi
a colorful celebration
with a night-long bonfire,
throwing a demon dummy
of Holika, dancing and tossing
organically produced pigments
which will not irritate eyes
and will wash off clothes.

Celebrants dance to Bollywood music,
chase each other with water
from squirt guns or buckets,
and multi-colored powers to coat
clothes and skin. Everyone
can come–Hindu or not
to eat Indian food, join in the fun.

If you don't like hue-splashes
in the face or elsewhere
"Bura na mano. Holi hai."
"Don't get offended, it's Holi."

Too sore-kneed to dance,
I would love to sprinkle color
and goodness in a joyful spring romp
of song, dance and play.
I will celebrate Holi in choreographed words.

Spring

Easter tree
dangles pastel plastic eggs
in gusty air

pink magnolia blossoms
mosaic sky
and ground

petals fringe sidewalks
blow to streets
brown on ground

don't dye eggs
unless you eat them
bunny's hopping mad

after Easter
bunnies deliver bunnies
not eggs

bunnies celebrate
spring with
a bun dance

Winged-Ones On My Mind

I can see birds in changeable air
on flexible tree limbs and taut telephone wire,
pecking polluted lawn unaware I'm there,
but they're not the winged-ones I desire.

I would like to see fairies flitting about,
not butterflies or winged bugs.
Fairies are here I have little doubt,
probably lassoing worms and slugs.

If fairies are real in some dimension
and imagination reflects in this realm,
I'd like to expand my comprehension
and put fairies back at their helm.

This extends to angels as well.
Images of them are world-wide.
Think of the mysteries they could tell
and all the guidelines they could provide.

There is something about wings.
They lift delight and insight—
an elevation which brings
us closer to joy and the light.

I want to know all exist
not just believe they might be real.
Somehow I just can't resist
any other-worldly appeal.

Spring Angel

Instead of a secular Easter Bunny
carrying pagan egg tradition
why not a Spring Angel–
a symbol in many faiths?

Angels can carry eggs.
Flying is faster than hopping.
Angels can design artistic eggs
without animal donations.
Maybe holographic eggs
glowing ethereal images.

Angels can be like a spring Santa
filling baskets with small surprises.
They can create their own gifts
or assist humans toward
joyful, healthy selections.
Dark chocolate is my personal request.

Maybe angels will have fairy assistants
to tend buds, bulbs to bloom.
All the tulips, daffodils, forsythia
flowering plums and cherries bursting
open to the touch of winged-ones
for the enjoyment of pedestrian species.

Angels should not be a seasonal tradition
but an all-year round phenomenon.
Light is needed beyond the sun
and artificial light creations.
Let halos be tossed to Earthling heads.
Let angels bring music, joy and peace
and let it all begin in spring
when renewal is the essence of all spirits.

Spring angels are eternal
beyond the energizer bunny.
Bunnies of imagination and fertile abundance
hop aside, take a vacation, retire–
angels are bringing it!

Santas and Easter Bunnies

Where does the Easter Bunny go
after hopping all over the place
delivering decorated eggs
for baskets, egg hunts and rolls?

Does EB have to lay-off fairies
from the egg assembly line?
Paws do not have the delicacy
of fingers.   EB must have help.

Does EB take a vacation
with abundant family
at some hole in the wall
or hop a jet to sunny climes?

Santa Claus goes to the North Pole
to re-join Mrs. Claus.
His elves barely pause production
since the diverse demands for gifts
keeps the Nordic economy
going all year.

Santa's sleigh has more capacity
than a measly basket.
His reindeer-powered sleigh
has much more room
and can deliver the goods faster
than a hopping basket-carrier.

The Easter Bunny must rely
on a whole batch of bunnies
hopping to it
on their special day.

Santas and Easter bunnies
both work secularized holidays.
These rituals transformed
from ancient traditions
of rebirth and renewal
evoke magic and mystery,
provoke imaginative leaps
and individual faith,
remain beacons of light
as ephemeral and eternal
as jack-o-lanterns.

Santas and Easter Bunnies
visit our hearts,
reside in us with wonder,
joy and seasonal delight.

When I spot their miniature replicas
around my home, I smile
and make sure
stockings and baskets
are ready on time.

Blurry Backyard

my cataracts are still ripening
with the spring flowers
shrouded by fog.

red rhodies with all the moist green
a Christmas palette
with fog-frost patina

clarity of vision elusive today
blurred by tired eyes
and dampening weather

fog must rise sometime
sun brighten outlook
now I face a frosty mirror

Time to Return to the Garden

Weather's warmed
the sky clear
I have no excuse
not to meditate in the backyard.

The pinks and reds blooming
along the street
have leaked to red azaleas
along the fence.

I should get my camp chair,
water and notepad to go
get distracted in spring.
But I check my list for today.

Already I skipped exercise
as I need to do a major cleanup
and set up four judging stations
for the Youth Poetry Contest.

I need to get the forms to fill out
in four categories in place
with the poems on the tables.
Set up snacks away from the poems.

I have a poetry workshop to lead
beforehand which I need to prepare for.
Lugging chairs around, paper piles,
respond to e-mails...

I look into the verdant yard
It would be a great place to release stress.
But it will have to be tomorrow.
Today I will try for a nap.

On a Gray April Day

driving in gully-washer
hail pelts windshield
damp chill carries inside
red cape and upping heat
can't warm anxious heart

driving from massage
road slick as lubed muscle
flesh rubbed and warmed
my belly flab stimulated to flow
energetic blood in uptight body

driving from exercise
bands, balls, weights
gray/white hair on bobbing heads
Silver Sneakers not slippers
Cinderellas without princes

Sitting at computer
peeking at the keys
I touch black and white thoughts
hoping for technicolor
of a sunny day

Momentary Stays

Sun sinks in the west.
I sit in quivery shade.
Wind shuffles leaves.

Red cape snuggles warmth.
Wind chimes sway.
I relax after Scrabble, moving my pen.

We played Scrabble on the table
sprawling words without board, not keeping score.
Letters attached like leaves to branches.

Now like lint from sky's fabric,
bugs buzz by, floating fuzzy seeds
without direction unlike Scrabble tiles.

Everything seeks a place—
momentary before
changes propel movement.

Nobody Sees a Flower

*Nobody sees a flower–really–it is so small–we haven't time–and to see takes
time like to have a friend takes time.* Georgia O'Keefe

Serial Scrabble players gather to play.
One brings her hand-picked bouquet,
floral fragrance still upon her hands.
Old friends whose camaraderie expands
in windowed room with backyard view
charming college teachers' milieu.

A lone robin pecks the ground
no other birds around.
A purple rhododendron hides
in under-story, resides
near fence near white iris
It is planted there I guess.
to be near pink azaleas and red
rhododendron for contrast instead
of the berry patches near by—
a lovely palette for those who fly.

The Scrabble cronies don't keep score,
play with words, reconnect once more.
On the table two bouquets- one real
the other artificial sunflowers— not ideal
but my mother kept plastic flowers or silk
and I have some blooms of the same ilk.
They add color and will not fade
like some friendships we have made.

Three buttercups spread out and yawn
yellow in a weedy, green, butch-cut lawn.
Clover clump of lavender in niche of wall
hardly draws any attention at all.
The cut flowers on the table bend.
Many varieties vanish in the end
unlike these friendships flourishing
because these players are nourishing
seeds of sharing over time and play
together in a supportive way.

Bird Battles

Those bothersome birds are back.
A friends says they are orioles not jays.
Ripening cherries are under attack
helpless to the robbers' ways.
They came during a speck of sun.
The bird battles have begun.

A friends says they are orioles not jays
and she is a birder with experienced eyes.
I am a novice at bird traits and ways.
Poor cherries don't stand a chance. Sighs
of defeat for the victims and us.
I wish there would not be such a fuss.

Ripening cherries are under attack
before they are barely pink.
Not now ready for a human snack,
but just the right hue the birds think.
To them cherries' taste is yummy
and just right for their tummy.

Helpless to the robbers ways
I stare out the window. Once more
we'll need nets, shiny pans, but no sprays–
we've been in this battle before.
Noise, nets, cats, shiny things don't work.
But from our duties will we shirk?

They came during a speck of sun
just the first flock to arrive.
This conflict they have already won.
The young cherries will not survive.
They get eaten by people or bird
so this skirmish to them is just absurd.

The bird battles have begun.
I guess we could just share.
We'd rather get other things done.
We are getting too old to care
who picks and pecks at the tree.
I just know it won't be me.

Bird Watching

When I sit in the backyard, birds
squawk in the distance telling each other
I am too close to the ripening cherry tree.

Perhaps their cherry GPS calls
other birds to feed. At any rate
I see more birds from the window.

I stopped trying the dissuade the birds
from pesticide-free cherries. Most cherries
are higher than any stable ladder we own.

To me cherries are an unreachable snack,
glossy ornaments on a Christmas tree,
shiny marbles or bright buttons.

Branches dance as birds land
and sway in wind. I've seen crows on the treetop,
starlings, scrub jays, stellar jays, robins on lower limbs.

Cherry pits pebble the lawn.
Their chewed flesh squishes under foot,
strewn beneath the tree in shadow.

Friends and I watch birds through windows
while playing Scrabble or during writing groups.
Bird watchers identify the visitors.

They check their bird books to see
if it's a cowbird or female starling, stellar
or scrub jay, count cherries a crow eats (9).

A friend said, "Maybe birds are E.T.'s."
Hmm, would different bird species
be from different alien races? If so, whose?

Would they solidify when they are in our realm
into birds? Would they have a penchant for cherries?
Would cherries be a diversion from dry birdseed?

Would they spy on us- wire-tap through their feet
on transmission lines? Would they monitor electronic messages?
Hmm, they would be great surveillance –flock or solo.

Would these high-fliers, mostly fair weather friends or foe,
find tinier targets and nooks than planes or drones? Would
they flock in formations to relay messages? Beam info upwards?

Would they just come here on vacation to enjoy
the natural and unnatural beauty of the planet? Would
they come because they are curious or for reconnaissance?

Would they feel free to fly despite
long-limbed creatures who shoo and shoot,
cats who chase and capture?

Would E.T. transform into birds leaving
their cumbersome gear onboard their heavy transports?
Would they hologram a new identity?

Would they be multidimensional, capable
of changing shape, space and density when
faced with earthly challenges?

Would they tip-toe on wire like an aerialist,
notate the wire-staff lines into music,
snatch bugs and cherries from trees or ground?

Birds have otherworldly connections in myths as messengers,
special knowledge in symbology, folk and fairy tales,
Egyptian reincarnation. Maybe they have always been E.T.s

I guess it would not matter to me if they were E.T.s.
I'm willing to witness their performances
and share the stage with the flying folk.

But it would be nice if they would eat high on the treetop
and leave a few cherries on lower branches for us.
Chance of that is about the same as birds being E.T.s.

Well, blueberries and strawberries are not ripe yet.

Cosmic GPS

A robin bashed a reddish breast
against the front window three times
before perching on a holly bough.
Below, smaller black birds poke grass.

Wings flutter frantically
against glass, possibly pursuing
a reflection of the holly tree
the robin rested upon.

Birds navigate magnetic migrations
with celestial cues to find landings.
What led this robin to thrust
its body in such futile pursuit?

Are all conscious beings guided
from another dimension with unseen creators
filtering thoughts and actions
into various parts of our brain?

Are our bodies subject to cosmic directional systems
beamed to us to perform until our equipment expires?
How much independent thought do we generate?
Many great minds credit channeling for their genius,

Are we in some video game, cosmic entertainment
or experiment, some computerized simulation?
Are we pushing the controls or are other entities?
Do we really have a soul in charge? Free will?

The battering-ram-bird sits stunned
on the branch. Dark birds swirl underneath
like orbiting planets around a sun.
Holly berries the stars.

The Robin Returns

Robin breast-bumped against the pane.
Several morning beak and calls
with wings whopping glass

Today without satellite mini-black birds,
alone the robin confronts a collage
in a holly tree reflection.

What makes the bird leave a holly bough
for an illusion when the real tree
is beneath feet's grip?

The window reflects the holly tree,
a tall conifer, unlit electric candle,
miniature angels dangling from the ceiling

Angels in shadow with slight glitters
could be mistaken for birds
glimmering in sunlight.

Is robin lonely or seeking holly berries?
Birds can be messengers from the departed.
Black birds dart before me in significant times.

The robin perched on another branch,
a companion holly tree with white-etched leaves.
A few un-clipped or un-snipped berries remain,

My horoscope said my worries will dissipate
with confidence and solace will come
in sensitive communication with friend or lover.

Perhaps the robin is trying to get my attention
prying, prodding me into connection
with those whose tears appear berry red.

Visitations

...Poetry is that/which arrives at the intellect/by way of the heart.
R.S. Thomas "Don't Ask Me..."

A bobbing robin nibbles
dropped cherries in the shade.
What if an E.T. beamed in
on sun-rays like birds.

I expect an Alien would be
much more intelligent than I am
but would this otherworldly creature
have a heart or emotional equivalent?

E.T. could be a gender-less machine,
automaton, hybrid, puny Gray
or a massive monster...unimaginable.

A blue jay grounds, stops
for a cherry snack, flies away
with a mouthful.

No space craft could fit in our backyard
so a representative would have to teleport.
How would we communicate? Is there
a cosmic telepathy that would connect us?

Would it be mathematical as scientists
claim all the universe understands
or would it be words?

I would like to think this being
expresses poetry. If there is
music of the spheres, maybe
we'd compose lyrics for universal songs.

A bobbling brownish starling lands
on a cherry branch until a sky-blue scrub jay
chases the darkling away.

How could I attract cosmic
diversity into my life?
How could my poetry become
more universal?
How could I make an encounter
enlightening and loving?

Spring breezes rustle branches
reaching toward sunlight.
My restless soul ponders
sky's wondrous possibilities.

For now I watch the rhythms of shadows
in dancing sun blotted by night–later.
My imagination will have to populate
the backyard with alien aerial visitors.
I'll conjure congenial poets
(I hope they do not find me repulsive).

But perhaps they are already here
grounded like me.
Is the hose like a string in bio-networks
of group-think some researchers
predict space travelers would create?
Or are they samara-like starseeds,
DNA bacteria buds, electronic nano-bits
already planted seeking fertile earth.

Perhaps I should envision
I am Earth-evolved star-spawn
larger visible cosmic folk pick up
so I could tag-a-long
encrypting the multiverse
poetically.

Samaras

On my blue chair under the overhang
is a solitary samara of undetermined origin
unseen by the scattered whirligigs below
on a patio of pavers encrusted with moss.

Across the patio spiders, ants and flies crawl
take smoother short-cut to grass. Ants are faster,
Tiny legs navigate well over rough terrain. Some fly.
Why are they black? To look like shadows of themselves?

Beige mini-helicopters like veiny half-wings—
windblown design and intention.
swept off the roof by roofers
or drifted by the winds, can't move.

I open a winged achene with an aery green seed inside
and toss it over the grounded bugs like a parent tree
toward scraggly lush lawn,
hoping it is not too late to sprout.

But I noticed the seed was crushed,
stepped upon. I open another unblemished,
papery whirlybird (also called key) and toss seed.
Dried winged ones still spin-fly to ground.

Water Babies

We are all water babies. We came into this world in water. Laughter may be your cheapest medicine but your best and first medicine is water. Guard it with your life. Without it, we can't live.

Grandmother Agnes Baker Pilgrim of Confederated Tribes of Siletz

This morning's newspaper account
of the Dalai Lama's visit to Oregon
contained a comment by Agnes Baker Pilgrim:
we are all water babies.

As I dressed to go into the backyard
to get some rays and inspiration,
I decided to wear a pro-blue statement
under azure sky in backyard
filled with green and reddish-toned growth.
I put on blue socks, slacks, underwear;
blue sweatshirt with hunchbacked, flute-playing Kopopelli
blue eye-lace for blue-rimmed glasses,
blue-beaded band from Kenya over my black watch.

Under sunny skies
carrying water in a dark blue glass
for one pocket of my blue camp chair
and mobile phone in other pocket
I ponder water babies.

Children presented white lilies to the Dalai Lama.
He presented a khata, a white welcome scarf
to Portland's mayor.
Politicians can work for the environment,
protect the Columbia River and gorge from coal trains.
protect us all from pollution.
According to The Oregonian
the interfaith religious leaders on stage
espoused stewardship of the environment.
The Dalai Lama said spiritual or not
we must all act to protect and preserve the Earth.

He recalled his childhood in Tibet with clear streams.
He was 24 when he went to India before he knew
some water is not drinkable. He learned
about water pollution, endangered species
and environmental threats due to consumption.
He went on to talk about the Earth, enlightenment, education,
mother's love, oneness, compassion, kindness.

But my thoughts returned to the water babies image.
Recently I left pool exercise mostly because
of poor water quality and wondered
how many pure pools can teach water babies to swim.

We seek Goldilocks planets hosting water for life
when we must leave our damaged, perhaps water-less planet.
We have ecological responsibility now.
Often-rainy Oregon is having a sunny spring.
Many Oregonians pray for rain,
implore winter-chaser, spring-bringer Kokopelli
to sustain life-giving blessings
of water and fertility.

When in sun, my red cape hangs
on the blue chair-back like a stop sign
red light–a warning to pursue blue waters.

When I move to chilly gable's shade,
my red cape drapes over my shoulders
urges me to shoulder stewardship.

I look at the cloudless sky
floating white seed-puffs seeking
moist landings beside dried samaras
swept from the roof by recent roofers
or air-drifters to grass and patio.
I consider watering the backyard,
glance at unfilled, small, sideways,
shallow plastic pool
and hope somewhere
in clean water deep enough
all water babies learn to swim.

Life After Life

With respect for science and the scope for knowledge, certain types of
phenomena are beyond their scope. The fact that science cannot evaluate an
idea is not the same as science disproving it. Dalai Lama

Shaded by a hazelnut tree,
two dandelions at my feet,
a silent fly walks a stalk of grass.

Amid splendor of spring- splashes of rhododendron
purple clover and azaleas
greening grass and leaves, steady evergreens,

neighbors mow lawns. Birds chat.
I sit and hold newspaper clippings of Dalai Lama
while sipping cold tea.

In Eugene 11,000 people pass through security
to hear the Dalai Lama speak of one world, one humanity.
We build a peaceful world from individual's inner peace.

In Portland at a Life After Life symposium
Maitripa College students kneel on meditation benches, chant
in Tibetan, images of beauty: star, lamp flame, dewdrop, lightning flash.

Quietly, faith incarnate Tenzin Gyato
14th reincarnation of Dalai Lama enters quietly and bows.
He will speak after Dr. Eben Alexander.

Dr. Alexander experienced "Proof of Heaven:
A Neurosurgeon's Journey in the Afterlife".
His neocortex shut down in a near-death event.

"Our souls come back again and again" he says.
The Dalai Lama nodded affirmatively.
Many believe in reincarnation regardless of religious affiliation.

The Dalai Lama joked about the appeal of centuries
of rest even if it happens to be in a coffin,
says brain research reveals mysteries:

gap between reality and appearances
idea of impermanence and role of emotions.
Examine texts with a critical eye. He left saying "See you again."

Medium Teresa Caputo had her brain scanned
and different areas of her brain activate when she contacts
the dead in another dimension

I have experienced contact with beloveds
who are exploring other real estate.
A channeler said I have 14 simultaneous lives now.

My hand shadows my sunshined notebook page.
I stuff newspaper articles in chair pocket with mobile phone.
I ponder multiple possibilities.

I would be an inept Buddhist.
My knees could not tolerate meditation benches
My red cape is shorter than the Dalai Lama's.

I have more of a Buddha belly
than the 77 year old man, four years my elder.
Both of us bespectacled, balding, like caps and wear red garments,
Life after live is a overwhelming concept.
My 14 simultaneous lives are unfathomable, even this earthly one.
What am I doing elsewhere and lives throughout time?

Is there an end-date to reincarnations?
When did my many lives begin?
How many places in the multiverse are available?

I have no problem with alien life, multi-dimensional lives,
reincarnation, but contemplating all past and possible lives
is beyond my Earth-borne brain wired to the multiverse–

currently disconnected.

Mother's Day

Be a compassionate person, not necessarily a religious believer. Dalai Lama

Mother's Day we gave our mother called Honey, pansies.
There are only mono-toned patches of color in our yard.
Perhaps I should plant pansies in my entry planters.

The Dalai Lama suggests mothers should become leaders
because of their empathy and compassion, encourage trust,
give affection and love, reduce insecurity and fear in their children.

Well, the Earth is our home. Each individual is responsible
to sustain the environment, show loving kindness,
give children and young people a sense of hope.

He says, we must build an economy not based on unlimited growth
and unlimited consumption. A peaceful world.
Scorn wealth and material consumption as means to true happiness.

Khatas, the white silk scarf, symbol of unity and pure hearts
a Blazers cap and basketball jersey were gifts to the Dalai Lama.
He said the jersey was of no use, but the cap very useful.

As I sit in my blue chair gazing at the garden I remember
the Dalai Lama told the crowd to keep this scarf.
"Unity and happiness must be part of your life now."

My red cape spills like a broken heart,
bloody, flannel not silk
weighing heavy on my shoulders.

I take off my cape, walk to our garage,
climb in True Blue, my Geo Metro,
leave to buy some pansies to plant.

The Eternal Child

Beyond the indoor room's window
I stare at the backyard jostling for growth.
Sidewalk-chunk wall grimaces at overcast morning.

My red cape snuggles and warms me.
but a recurrent dream disturbs the quiet
this chilly spring day.

I recall no color or movement in the dream
except for breathing from this dormant baby
I cradle in my arms. The baby is not just sleeping.

Swathed in a blanket, the baby is motionless—
the length of my forearm. A baby bundle I sense
will not walk, talk, see or hear for a long while.

This infant is alive but unresponsive,
the size of a tightly packed pocketbook.
I do not know the gender or how we are connected.

What is the meaning of this baby bond?
A child I did not conceive this life time?.
What message should I get from this coma-child?

Is the baby incubating for delivery in some dimension?
Am I a volunteer infant-holder in another realm? On dream duty?
Revived newborn recovering between lives on the Other Side?

Who were the parents?   Somehow I know
the baby is waiting for delivery
to someone, sometime, somewhere.

In the backyard buds, blooms and blades
burst and inch growth, throb with life
I'm troubled by an eternal baby I'm too old to berth.

My black "She Who Watches" petroglyph
tee shirt and black sweat pants
hide under my red cape. I appear an unmarked rock.

I look through the window, like at a garden nursery, yet
my mind imagines a hospital nursery of swaddled newborns.
I remember a solo baby cuddled in my arms— still as stone.

Unmasking
The world will present itself to you for its unmasking. Franz Kafka

Dragging a camp chair from the patio to backyard,
I notice seed pods gathered in the seat,
remove the wind-blown debris to the lawn.

Four buttercups dim in nearby shadows.
Tree shade leaning west sways in breeze.
Roof dark traces cast still and sharp-edged.

Sun will unmask the shadowed lawn
change the shadow at my feet
spread before me like an inkblot.

Birds and planes heard but not seen
through the tree's canopies.
Weeds camouflaged in grass.

A tie-dye cap covers my head.
Blue case awaits camp chair's folding.
Red cape towels my exercised, achy body.

Uncovering what is hidden brings
turbulent thoughts churning inside my scull—
silent screams. I watch what is outside of me.

Buds eager to reveal petals.
Dandelion puffs deliver seed. Seeds want to pop open.
Aerial orts seek ground.

Dropped pen cap lost in lawn–
habitat for some bugs? What lurks in compost heap
beneath bark, under pavers, underground?
What is under my feet seeking Gaia's chi?
What is beyond seeable sky– unknowable dimensions,
multiverse, particle zoo.

I toast in sun. Macro and micro worlds
concealed by my limited equipment.
Glasses darken to darkle surroundings.

I am part of a mysterious, mystical masquerade.
construct facades to block darkness and project light,
hide actions and interactions, controlled by fear and love.

I crumble a dark chocolate candy wrapper
stuff it into the chair pocket.
message unread.

Curiosity un-crumbles the wad.
It reads "Relaxation by chocolate". I laugh.
Sun-unmelted chocolate melts in my mouth.

With all the stress in the world
I want to coat a layer of hope.
I carry my cape inside on my arm - my soft shield.

Muddled Meditation

Whenever I can contemplate
I try to find a comfy spot.
Backyard vistas lure my focus.
Distracted by details, I try
to think cosmically inward, but
backyard vistas lure my focus.
I try to find a comfy spot
whenever I can contemplate.

Vibes

As I sit sluggishly in the backyard camp chair
hoping for a jolt of Gaia energy juice,
I think of the vibrational levels I am supposedly
to lure through my lymphs to my brain
to ascend to higher vibrational levels.

My soul can't ascend at my own rate
and stay on my own path without some effort on my part.
I need to develop my resistant consciousness
and raise my vibrational signatures
to a higher level of intensity. Seems doubtful.

Supposedly this is universal law
for reaching higher meanings
and values for soul progress.
Despite all my reading and sucking up
soul vibes through soles of my feet– I'm waiting,

I need some "upstepping" of both my body
and consciousness if I am to achieve
the divine connection, my I AM perfection.
This effort could bring me to my cosmic "Home".
I've never been a perfectionist.

Yet I am part of All, a sentient soul
in a time/space reality. All things
animate and inanimate consist of light
and vibration at the subatomic level. The Creator
is the source of all beings, matter, energy, some say.

That is a lot of vibes for this vehicle .
Consciousness needs to deal with this crone
to interact with the environment, undergoing global warming,
adapting to density, speed and light.
until possibly enlightened to a transitional level.

Then I learn human bodies interface consciousness
within a limited range for living in an environment
of similar vibration. I need an energy infusion
to kick my consciousness higher and then maybe
when I transit to another realm I'll reach a higher vibe.

Right Now

Say you want to sing, Right now   Aaron Anstett

Say you want to sing or dance right now
or say something else, like a bird would do.
I'll sing. I know the lyrics. The tune escapes me.

A faint echo as though from deep in the valley
comes nearer now.
Ah, I hear the birds singing, calling.

I'm coming, carrying
the newly refurbished bird houses
so birds can sing on perches, balconies.

Is anyone listening?
My song echoes wildly through the room–
"stand against the wind."

My breath, the wind,
the draft under bird wings
they all exist right now.

Spirit brings us back to oneness
to ourselves,
to all that is.

One great symphony,
slightly out of tune,
yet the poet sings.

Flowerings

Three vases of artificial sunflowers inside
cannot compete with living flowers in the backyard
but they will linger longer without bugs or scent.

Some people plant fake flowers outside
but if in communal living just have to keep
the flowers rotated to the season.

Some people actually water these plastic
or silk clones, damaging some
in this futile process.

My mother made floral seasonal wreathes
with silk blooms and recycled
bouquets perfect for any occasion.

My non-exhaling flowers get dusty
and I do not have enough for seasonal exchanges.
When they are tended for what I intend, they are beautiful.

Can't we enjoy any floral arrangements?
Animate or inanimate we're all the same
at the subatomic level.

Fasting

Anything else you're interested in is not going to happen if you can't breathe the air and drink the water. Don't sit this one out. Do something.
Carl Sagan

Sitting in the camp chair
blue as the spring sky,
sipping a water bottle,
I remember to wear sun screen
for my backyard meditations.
Previously without face protection,
my thought-provoking sessions
probably lead to the activation
of a nose carcinoma,
now removed.
I mended after a series
of colorful patterned bandages.

My row of scar bumps
remind me to carbonfast
and be aware of climate change,
my surroundings, my responsibility
as a steward of the Earth.

We try to recycle, not use
poisonous sprays; conserve water,
We do not smoke, but pollute the air
with our efficient cars.
We are aware we need to do our best
in our home and whatever we do.

Visions of smog, acidifying garbage dump oceans,
coal trains, toxic chemical carrying transports,
exploding bombs, radiation, spills
of lethal materials....the list goes on.
Even with a carbonfast and purifying water
the damage stays in the seas and air.
We need to make Earth sustainable
before we can journey to the stars.

But with the lusty lawn thrusting green,
the pastel cherry, apple, plums blossoms,
fluted daffodils renewing color and hope,
for a few minutes I can enjoy,
drink in un-blurred beauty
and resolve to try to keep a watered world
un-bandaged and breathing.

Backyard in May

red azaleas
under soggy clouds
await sun-kissed glow

azaleas sprawl
over wooden fence
sieve wind

pink and red rhodies
buffer azaleas
merge boundaries

unmown grass bends
awaits mower
and a butch-cut

moist, fragrant, vibrant
before petals fall–
lips kissing earth

This Memorial Day

*When you cling to values you know are true, / like family, God, the red,
white and blue./ It's your fortress 'gainst indoctrination/when flood waters
rise, breaking mind levee/you go on, though the standard heavy/But you
live in confirmed desperation...*   Major General John Borling
"Taps on the Walls: Poems from the Hanoi Hilton"

Here in our backyard a patch of pale white iris
beside blushing azaleas and rhododendrons
recall unfolding bandages and oozing wounds.

Today was called Decoration Day because
fresh flowers would be in bloom
to decorate the graves of soldiers.

Cherries ripen toward red in various hues.
Nourishing hazelnut, pear, peach and apple trees
less obviously bearing fruit.

The backyard is a battlefield
for exploding buds and blooms, blasting bugs
and pollen, skirmishes of cats.

My red cape scarf snapped around my neck,
I sit in a blue camp chair
writing on a blank white page.

An overcast day dawns
awaits armistice of sun
after a rainy night.

Elsewhere a local high school bomb plot aborted,
patriots parade, shoppers seek sales, sports entertain,
mourners attend observances or take mini-vacations.

Domestic and foreign wars rage.
Politicians debate drones, security sensors,
satellites, surveillance cameras, fences, costs of wars.

Recent random acts of natural and un-natural tragedies
require solace: Oklahoma tornado, Superstorm Sandy
Boston Marathon attacks, Newtown...

We will have a moment of silence
in remembrance of the fallen
as living veterans endure medical claims backlog.

We have wars on crime, drugs, diseases,
homelessness, inequality, terrorism,
global warming, issue or cause of the month.

Poetry saved Borling through 6 ½ years
as POW in a North Vietnamese prison camp
by memorizing his experiences in poems.

Can all this carnage and violence
be healed by remembering, humor,
compassion as well as poetry?

Here as I face backyard red/white flowers and write,
our rock wall reminds me of tombstones. But
in the front yard we have yellow roses and purple clematis.

Everywhere most people remember love,
hope for rainbows and peace.
My red cape bleeds like a bloody flag.

Re-Roofing

ladders and cranes
carry materials to stripped roof
rain or sunshine

reindeer-roofers prance
on rooftop, pound shingles
gifts from Santa

tap, tap, tap roofer elves
work to hip hop music
move spritely

shadows flash by skylights
to build a new sun tunnel
in living room

new fascia board peaks
replace dry-rotted ones
await paint

shingles blend in fog
reflect sun prepared
for all seasons

Replacing Our Roof

When I welcomed the roofers
to use our bathrooms
I did not expect a pee parade
flies unzipped dashing down the hall
toilet seats left up
slippery stocking feet in contrast
to the elephant-hoofed clomping on the roof.

When the crane arrives
plopping bundles of shingles overhead with sonic booms,
when the tap, tap, tapping of roofer elves
wielding heavy hammers and staple guns
tromping to blaring hip hip music.
I did not expect the ripping, tearing and tossing,
the loud banter and swearing, the detritus below.

When they worked near existing skylights
debris fell on the kitchen surfaces
and in the room full of thousands of angels
I did not expect two decapitated angels
and plaster orts littering floor like clumped artificial snow.
They do not clean up.

When they commandeered the garage
and held it hostage with their supplies,
when they made our exits heads-up, hazardous zones,
when they left a crust of roof dandruff on the washer and dryer
and I could not use either dirtied machine due to their equipment
blocking access and sucking electricity from the sockets
until they exploded my lunch in the microwave in a surge
interrupting power and destroying the microwave
I was beginning to feel captive and unsafe in my home.

When the writers and Scrabble players
came over to word-play amid the fallen angels
I wondered if the cursing roofers
would fall through the skylight or dribble more white ceiling flakes
to punctuate our pages or leave pieces on the Scrabble board.

When I realized they would be back next week to finish the roof
paint replaced dry-rotted fascia boards, put in the sun tunnel
install two windows in more renovations
and over the weekend an exposed area leaked inside
during a rain storm, I knew these spidery men
were not through webbing the roof.
I had to do some revisionist thinking
perhaps escape into fantasy.
These reindeer-roofers prancing on my roof
were not bright gifts from Santa but Satan.
I will tell my guests
amid the clamor and debris
to envision fairy dust or rogue stardust sprinklings,
hammers are transforming magical wands
music is wind chimes or
a friend's roofer who sang romantic love songs in Spanish
gathering neighboring fans as he worked.

When alone in the chaos of my disheveled home,
furniture and decor misplaced to provide space
for these clodhoppers, bellowing Thors,
I will close doors and screen the un-zipped men
blast the TV or hover over my computer
wearing earplugs.

Replacing Their Roof

Gray reflective roof for two geezers.
The old man prances around like a kangaroo
opening garage doors for our gear,
clearing out the rafters for Habitat for Humanity.
He knows what we need to do.

The old lady plays Scrabble
and writes with friends in a room
full of angels–and gets pissed
when two fall and break.
The old man repairs them.

When we head for the bathroom
which she said we were welcome to use
we find small stuffed bunnies and chickens
staring at us from the toilet top and counters.
She puts down the toilet seat after we leave.

We have overheard her telling friends
she finds our music blaring and jarring,
our hammering annoying
and just walking on the roof–like elephants.
She overhears swearing.

We did blow up her lunch in the microwave
in a power surge, block her washer and drier
with our equipment, restricting access,
leave roof dirt on top of the machines,
but we usually wore socks when indoors.

They are like Jack Spratt and his wife.
He climbs up the ladder to inspect our work
while she stays inside with mixed-seasonal
decorations, some of which are still Christmas,
playing word-games, writing poems–complaining.

The shingles match the clouds this rainy day.
They reflect the sun, but not today.
She glows about the new sun tunnel just installed
but does not mention the new roof sheltering them.
To her, we are like carpenter ants found inside their siding,
                    a nuisance.

Wonderlings

On the last day in May I sit under a ripening cherry tree,
face our home whose windows stare at me, watch my husband
fiddle on the roof, painting boards from a recent renovation.

The only other creatures I see in the yard are fly-by insects.
I hear distant birds, but what if other cosmic kith or kinds lurk
unseen— extra-terrestrials or ultra-terrestrials.

They are beyond my ken with this 3-D earthbound body.
I can't detect their higher frequencies with this sensing equipment.
The predicted 5th dimensional shift hasn't happened here.

This is probably not a hot spot for Supernaturals.
More lush and interesting stops exist elsewhere. I'm not much
to gawk at with over-used parts. But I hope they'd enjoy the flowers.

Some speculate 33 is ultimate consciousness (not me)
and that E.T.'s enter star gates or portals on the 33rd latitude
where Roswell and Mt. Herman reside. I'm near 45th.

These cosmic travelers could visit many dimensions,
come as holograms, transform Earthlings, blip in and out
of this dimension like some say Big Foot does.

There are scientific, metaphysical and theological reasons
why this backyard might not be the best choice for them.
But I welcome them sight unseen.

What fun to think fairies flit among flowers to string sounds,
retreat to mounds or underground residences to dance and re-troop.
Once I believed they did. Devas would care more about vegetation.

What an honor to think aliens would come to witness here!
They would see our hand-built sidewalk-chunk wall and chuckle
after credited for ancient sonar and high-tech construction world-wide.

From alien intelligence I could learn all about the cosmos—
Earthlings' part in ALL. Perhaps we are cosmic cousins
with DNA left from other encounters and they came to check us out.

What about a host of angels having a conclave somewhere?
A few could stop by to pick up my guardian angels for a reunion,
leaving me earthbound, alone in my own time.

Islamic writing angels would be great possible stand-ins.
Two Kiraman Katibin: "noble recorders", "honorable scribes"
named Raqib and Atid could perch on my shoulders temporarily.

Right shoulder angel records good deeds (better odds for Jannah, "heaven)
Left shoulder angel records bad deeds. (better odds for Jahannam, "hell")
People's lifelong actions, feelings and thoughts recorded for Allah's mercy.

Angels are part of the unseen world Muslims believe in.
Other religions believe in angels also. Perhaps they would be
my writing angels and help my muse jot down my earthly experiences.

But writing angels are not guardian angels called mu'aqqibat" or "followers"
who are front or back of people, so would not bestow any Islamic perks
to a non-believer while my non-denominational guardian angels are away.

I'm bopped from my reverie by an unseen treetop bird
dropping a chewed cherry on my knee to join
fallen cherries polka-dotting the lawn.

Or maybe it is otherworldly snackers shooting spit balls,
or should I get a pea-shooter to deter the birds?
I'll move into sunshine under wonderling-filled sky.

I'll share the yard with all-comers
from wherever– seen or unseen
even other people's pooping pets.

Time Flies

Time being, after all, only the current of the soul in its flow. D.H. Lawrence

Purple petals curl under rhododendron.
Lavender clematis now blanched spines.
White iris tanned beige.

Hues disappear, desiccate, fade, fall.
Grass will brown without summer watering.
Fruits and nuts such a short time to be delectable.

Frantic fly flits inside warm room
with backyard view, lands for respite
from swatter in only live plant— a Gerbera daisy.

Fly crawls up the shiny window.
hides in small wall and window rim
but cannot find an open outside door.

Fly wants the backyard breezes
not the stagnant air of this room,
but will the fly escape before its end time?

Solo fly does not seem in contact
with the other insects in our home
or disturb inhabitants like mosquitoes.

Now fly squeezes between screen and window,
clutches glass and resides un-swattable
but caged, unable to get free.

Birds and bugs hit the window time to time,
do not get trapped inside our lair.
Instantly our contact severs.

Inside insects share their short lives
sharing space briefly-
too short to ponder their intentions.

Flora and fauna everywhere have own showings,
coming and goings, alive like people—
part of cosmic oneness and wonder.

Melding into Summer
The left hand of darkness is light.   Ursula K. Le Guin

Dregs of spring
yield to fruits of summer.
Cherries picked over. Birds find fallen fruit.

Flowers fade and tan in sun.
Wind drops petals. Floral orts
shrivel on parched ground.

Leaves hide hazelnuts,
peaches, pears, apples–
slower to grow than cherries.

I sit in backyard wearing short-sleeved tee
not sweatshirts or long-sleeved shirts.
Red cape hangs on hook in hall.

My left hand writes in lined notebook.
My right hand lifts a water glass.
Sun warms to my core.

Daily subtle changes in backyard landscape
match my shifting mind-scape.
More light than darkness. More fruitful actions.

Meditating Under Cover

On this day of summer solstice.
under canopies of cherry, pear,
peach, plum, hazelnut and apple
I could meditate in sun-warmth outside.

I envision rejoining my Swedish relatives
celebrating midsummer
with floral head wreathes
and dancing around maypoles in June.

But since the removal of a skin cancer
I have been wary of soaking in sun
even with protective creams
so I have been contemplating indoors.

As I gaze at the leafy lace
on the lush lawn, I want to go outside
under cover of laden branches
and hope for some fruitful thought.

My arsy–varsy approach to meditation
does not provide me the focus I need.
Distracted by garden details or household decor,
my wandering thoughts go wayward.

Whether under my red cape when backyard's chilly
or lightly layered when it is warm
my thoughts scatter freely anywhere I am.
I can grok behind windows and under a roof.

Thinking about the sparge of stars,
I recklessly explore celestial possibilities,
ungrounded, uncovered, loosening boundaries
of where it is possible to dwell.

Now

"It's being here now that's important. There's no past and there's no future. Time is a very misleading thing. All there is ever, is the now. We can gain experience from the past, but we can't relive it; and we can hope for the future, but we don't know if there is one."   George Harrison

Now is a matter of interpretation not just time but current conditions.
There is now and again, now and then, nowadays to figure out.

If now is the fulcrum in a seesaw and the past weighs one end down
the future is up in the air. Where is the tipping point?

If now is the apex of a pyramid, the past could be an upward climb
and the future downward glide, but what are the criteria for how steps taken?

If now is a skyscraper and I am on the 73rd floor in one of the rooms,
I don't know how many floors are in the high-rise building. When do I move?

How long is now- an instant, very recent past of say a month, year?
Now is of the moment, immediate action, present time?

Is it an attitude more than time period? Under existing circumstances.
A command to hop to it. A bit of a bossy word.

Be in the present! Be in the now! As if we had a choice.
Now has no in it. What would the w stand for?

Now that I am pondering now sitting in a foldable chair
writing in a notebook in a sunny backyard. How long do I do so?

Now the hose draws a green line across the lawn–dormant.
Crows crunch cherries on the treetop. Active. Momentary.

Sedentary, I watch my surroundings, thinking rapid-fire.
My hand itches and twitches to capture now...and beyond.

Now could be gone before I can live or record it.
How inclusive is now-earthly, cosmic or just individual?

How quickly must I react to now? At my age I face
mobility and processing problems. But I'll try.

Now I can pay attention to the present,
informed by the past, hopeful for the future.

Sunglasses

Sunglasses mask eyes,
protect sun-starved sight.
Sunglasses are sunplastics
in many cases.

Sunglasses can change shade,
adapt to shifting light;
after weeks of gray skies
they can take a vacation.

Sunglasses can be high fashion–
colorful, designer frames
by names some people know
or dollar delights.

Sunglasses conceal crinkles and crow's feet
black eyes and bad make-up,
bruises and blemishes disguised
not just rose-colored eye-ware.

Sunglasses dim eyes of movie stars,
add mystery and danger to gangsters,
required gear for some scenarios
where true motives are hidden.

The Day After the Fourth of July

Heat wave waning. Parched yard.
We recently returned from weeks away.
Bees hover over clover.
Buttercups tower above untended ground.

Our fourth was quiet. Husband ill.
Local All-American Anyone Can Join,
Fabulous, Fantastic Fourth of July Parade;
and Red, White and Blues Festival–unseen.

Nearby, until midnight rowdy youth blasted fireworks.
Macy's biggest display choreographed by Usher
and PBS Capitol Fourth watched
in couch comfort.

Far-flung and nearby family elsewhere
contacted by text and phone.
Around the world turmoil and explosions
while we celebrate our freedom.

This morning a deer entered our suburban yard.
Bird-plucked cherries gone.. Not much to munch.
Where did the deer hide from yesterday's hoopla
and the temptations of barbecues and picnics.

Displaced deer moves on, joins another deer
chased from our neighbors' yard,
shouted at not to eat her roses.
They cross a dangerously busy street to where?

So many migrations. We download photos
from our trip to National Parks and Las Vegas.
Hot spots. Volcanic legacy. All the creatures
struggling to be here, risking to be free.

Our Orchard Patch Mid-July

-1-

Few
pears.
Peaches-
none this year.
Unpicked hazelnuts.
Fallen apples small and not sweet.

-2-

On
ground
berries–
blueberries,
Strawberries dwindling.
Mostly mowed lawn and leaves cling.

-3-

Tree
trunks
mat moss,
fungus splats.
Tufted textures on
top-heavy drooping canopy.

-4-

This
sun
season
our orchard
insecticide-free
struggles to push open and blush.

-5-

I
can
only
watch and wait.
Bird battles. Fruit ripe.
Bountiful harvests beyond hands.

Mid-July

Birds purloined our cherries.
Our plums like cherries on steroids.
Unripened apple crop avoids
beak-peckers and hand-pickers.
Strawberries and blueberries
hazelnuts and peaches
survive, out-wait outreaches
of persnickety birds and suburban slickers.

Cherry Pit Spitters

Cherry pits mowed into speckled lawn,
branches clasp dry, brown stems left.
No cherries remain to pit, pawn.
Bird battles over. We're bereft.
For weeks cherries ripened. We beseech
a share of crop just out of reach.

Branches clasp dry, brown stems left
like cherry bomb fireworks fuses.
But our hands are not as deft
as bird beak which uses
no other devices to extract pit,
as they quickly dispose of it.

No cherries remain to pit, pawn
on neighborly folks this year.
We harvested just a few, drawn
by hand, no mechanized shaker here.
We could only eat and spit
no time to pickle or cook a bit.

Bird battles over. We're bereft.
We conceded defeat and just shared.
No ladders high enough to prevent theft.
No grandchild climber who snared
cherries from treetop crown of crows
and other birds who pecked and chose.

For weeks cherries ripened, we beseech
gifts from fruitful trees, not ornamental.
Elsewhere cherry stoners and pitters leech
pit. Straws, paper clips fundamental
to extracting pits to spit or cook flesh
for baking pies or chew to refresh,

A share of crop just out of reach
keeps me from cherry pit spitters' contests.
Cherry— beauty and quick death symbol can teach
us to enjoy fruitfulness, make generous bequests
to be solid in our core and be a spitting image
of ripening goodness at any stage.

Today's Inventory

Ides of July in my front yard
four rogue deep lavender clematis
splay through the fence.
Light green holly berries
not yet blood-red.

In our cherry-picked backyard
we harvest plums- looking
like swollen bruises.
Un-sprayed blemished apples plump—
gobbets not ready.

On the computer the word of the day
is "fribble". E-mails sprawl
supportive and positive messages

At the store I bought a beaded lariat
to hold my reading glasses
to see things close to me.

In the morning newspaper–protests
over the Martin-Zimmerman case.
Where Zimmerman was lawfully
acquitted of shooting Martin.
Americans are taking stock
of their opinions of justice.
Both families had endangered sons.
One son was killed in Florida in 2013

In Tuscaloosa, Alabama in 1982
we waited for a jury
to hold a truck driver responsible
for running over our son
an exchange student from Oregon
while he pedaled his bicycle toward campus.
The jury called his death an accident.
The driver did not even get a traffic ticket.

The two cases have similar tallies.
Both happened in the South
and were tried by southern juries
who legally allowed adult killers
of teenage boys to escape responsibility.
Two older men killed two unarmed younger men.
who were alone and out of their home neighborhood.
Different weapons, a gun and a truck—
still two fatalities from fear or incompetence..

Our son probably never saw
nor touched his killer.
made only local news.
Martin's death spawned national protests
and national media coverage.
But all four men left heartache
and questions of injustice.

Families grieve over something
they cannot change.
Attitudes may not change to account
for the loss of a child.
Irreplaceable losses diminish our inventory
for as long as we believe they will.

Too Hot To Handle

As I sit in a camp chair in the backyard
I feel the heat of hell
rather than the warmth of heaven
on this unearthly hot day.

Some days meditation appears impossible.
Distractions of loved ones take focus
from my own spiritual contemplations.

Attempting to get it all together
I peruse seasonal changes:
        sun-bent leaves droop
        lone peach flushes
        plums plummet

To activate change to the way
of love, light and service
I need to transform
        greed to generosity
        anger to compassion
        ignorance to wisdom

Many earnest enlightened ones,
inwardly-oriented, give advice on situations
they have not experienced.
Unencumbered by family,
they proselytize their methods
of dealing with earthly life;
turn to converts for sustenance
as they do God's work.

Without their props and prompts
I rely on self-reliance and self-responsibility
when I can. I'm just fired up. Un-doused.

Much as I want to nourish my family tree
today I'd rather be
      a mute peach
      shaded by limp leaves
      hoping beloved plums
      hang on awhile longer
while it's so ungodly hot around here.

Sweating It Out

Sun-braising in the backyard in August
95 degree heat. Sweating.
Internally I am not sweating the little stuff
but some big stuff. Some hot stuff.
I am boiling inside and out. Hyperhidrous.

Iced tea to cool my insides.
Air-conditioning will quell obvious sweat.
But my brain still sweats drama
and trauma meditation won't tamp.
Fears and disappointments ooze.

Today is just a sweaty day.
Most of what I feel I can't control
or offer helpful feedback.
So why deal with useless sweat?
I'll envision a daydream in spring.

Paralysis

Experience is one of the forms of paralysis. Erik Satie

Which way to move, when to stand firm
immobilizes my thought and action.
Like the lone sunflower in our niche
of a clump of purple clover
I feel out of step, rooted.

Rain tamped some wildfires.
Days seesaw temperatures.
Violent news, Everything seems active
except me in my camp chair
wafting thought over the backyard.

I can't just sit here and do nothing
as my mind whirls. What will prompt
me to arise and sally forth
into some worthwhile endeavor?
Dark chocolate and then what?

Summer Song

Breeze brings clinking of wind chimes
Birds squawk and cheep in trees.
Neighbor dog barks. Sprinklers whoosh.
Planes, trains and cars rumble.

Air stirs with whirrs of fan.
Air-conditioner drones.
Refrigerator hums keeping things cool.
Feet tap wood floors. Slam doors.

Phones ring. TV chatters. Radio murmurs.
Electronics beep. Alarm clocks ring.
Fireworks boom. People talk—
All in their own rhythmic summer beat.

Peek-a-Boo Clematis

One day they seem dying, petals folded inward.
Next day some are openly blooming.
One day thriving, flashing purple.
Next day surviving as bowed in spines.
It is August and I have no idea
day to day what I will see—
how many blooms will be flourishing
surrounded by veiny vines.

My bursts of insights are similar.
I should understand the cycles
of fertility in growth and thought.
But if I truly did, I would not spend
so much time questioning why
and the why not responses
to the mysteries of life.

The clematis' stubborn insistence
to be seen at its best and worst
in spurts, could be some encouragement
to my endless quest for comprehension.
As I play peek-a-boo too, in and out
of creativity and attention, I will rely
on persistence of curiosity.
My clematis chums and I continue
to beat around the bush.

March on Washington: 50ᵗʰ Anniversary
August 28, 1963- August 28, 2013

The arc of the moral universe may bend toward justice, but it doesn't bend on its own.
President Barack Obama

August 1963 our firstborn son Kip was one month old.
We lived in a 17 foot travel trailer near Fort Lewis
Army Base in Washington where my husband
was an ROTC lieutenant conscripted for a war
he did not believe in. I taught sixth grade on the base.
It bothered me one of my students Andre, bright and black
could not plan on some colleges or go certain places
in the era of Jim Crow, Jew Quotas, racism,
the Cold War, threat of nuclear war,
Vietnam War, urban riots, the draft,
women's liberation, segregation, poverty,
hippies drop out, drug and gun deaths.
We escaped the military for graduate school
to become college professors.
We had a dream we believed in, like Martin Luther King Jr.

*This march and that speech changed America. It opened minds, they melted hearts,
and they moved millions.* President William Clinton

August 1982 our son was nineteen
on a student exchange in Tuscaloosa, Alabama.
A trucker ran him over while he biked to campus.
A southern jury determined it was an accident.
The trucker did not even receive a traffic ticket
for killing our son. Southern justice.
We lost faith in the American Dream
of justice for all. Miscarriage of justice continued,
despite some progress made in civil and voting rights.
Men went to the Moon, then Mars
to explore the universe . While on earth
we all exploited resources, overpopulated,
polluted, created autocratic, violent societies
with frustrated, muted, difficult dreams.

The good news is just as was true in 1963, we now have a choice. We can continue down the current path, in which the gears of this great democracy grind to a halt and our children accept a life of lower expectations where politics is a zero-sum game where a few do very well while struggling families of every race fight over a shrinking economic pie–that's one path. Or we can have the courage to change.
President Barack Obama

August 2013 Kip would have turned fifty.
Our other children and grandchildren face a diminished dream.
More wars struck— Iraq, Afghanistan, globally,
and Obama contemplates an attack on Syria.
Assassinations, illegal immigration, 9/11, drones,
Occupy, gap between rich and poor widening.
Still racism, sexism, LGBT oppression, out-sourcing,
educational and economic inequality, unpopular wars,
Tea Party, religious fundamentalism, privatization
terrorism, global warming, environmental degradation,
losing voting rights, holes in the safety net,
gun control out of control, school massacres,
lack of affordable health care and entitlements,
still no economic justice, no equality of opportunity.
We are told to keep our eye on the prize,
have courage, hope, wake up and change.
Martin Luther King lll says we can't give up
because we have come too far from where we started.
Jamie Foxx says it's time to stand up and renew this dream.
Martin Luther King Jr. stood for nonviolence
yet we use fighting words to deal with injustice.
We are in the valley surrounded by mountains to climb.
We have not reached the mountaintop.
King wanted us to judge people by the content
of their character, promote oneness and freedom.
"Let freedom ring" he said, but the Liberty Bell
still has a crack in it.

Trachle
1.an exhausted, bedraggled person. 2. to fatigue, tire, wear out.
Dictionary.com

Slumped in a camp chair in the backyard,
sunshine warming worn-out joints and muscles,
I envy the flitting birds attacking our cherries.

I drink a nourishing liquid lunch, too tired to cook.
After a very late out- of- town play last night
and a very early exercise class this morning — I'm trachle.

The new play Ithaka is a modernized Odysseus story
of a woman soldier returning from Afghanistan with PTSD
after a emotionally-draining, heart-wrenching loss of a friend and war.

Reading the morning newspaper exhausts me.
A nameless newborn found dead at a recycle center.
Middle East on fire. Washington D.C. stagnant. etc...

World-weary from all the violence and negativity
it is hard to move forward, carry on with optimism,
I must energize trachle, the word of this day.

More sluggish than a slug, I lumber inside
to take a nap, But my brain broils thought
and I look forward to tonight's play–out of town.

This new play of Ursula Le Guin's novel
Lefthand of Darkness features a frigid journey
on a icy, gender-bender planet Gethen.

Ithaka stands for "psychological development
and resultant knowledge." A longing for home.
A journey of adventure and discovery.

The lefthand of darkness is light.
The Ekumen want a peaceful federation
of 83 planets for trade, culture and knowledge.

Both plays portray long journeys of self-discovery.
I am a curious crone getting off the couch to gussy up.
"The play's the thing." "Eat my dust".

Mishpocha

> *an entire family network comprising of relatives by blood and marriage and sometimes including close friends, clan.*　Dictionary.com

Cherries on various branches of the family tree could symbolize mishpocha
but the terms for some rather complicated relationships is mind-boggling.
Relatives by blood or adoption can be named pretty well.
Grandma, Grandpa, cousin, niece, nephew, brother, sister, aunt, uncle.
But then it gets tricky. Second and third cousin. Some "removed".

What connection do you have to ex-partners' families?
Divorce the in-laws as well? Children's partners remarry.
Some bring additional children from previous marriages.
Grandchildren could have step and half siblings.
How do we address additional alliances?

Should we figure out terms beyond first names to include
children's temporary partnerships sometimes without marriage,
the children of our children's partners. For family parties
where do we draw the line? It is difficult enough without
including friends as part of your clan. Birthdays? Holidays?

Cherries change with the seasons. Fruit falls.
New fruit ripens. Blood connections unknown in some cases.
Genealogy could provide some surprising ancestry.
Some family members are not found. People come and go
in our lives, not necessarily leaving by death.

Some large families could be a quagmire. Some branches pruned.
Finding Swedish relatives and visiting them was a delight
and I do not worry about titles. They are my father's parents'
siblings' descendants, but they feel close not distant,
relatives connected by blood and family lore, e-mail as well.

Estrangements happen (cherry bombs).
We can be cherry pickers and cherish those we can pick.
Cherries do not fall far from the tree. We need to nourish
our family tree and hope for cherry jubilee.
We define our mishpocha and they define us.

Handling the Hazelnut Tree

Scrub jays and squirrels
attack our hazelnut tree.
Beaks and paws pluck filberts.

I watch them snatch nuts.
Human hands could wait
too long for this filbert frenzy.

They won't last long enough to drop.
Won't be in oils, flour, coffee or liqueur.
No pralines, Nutella or with chocolate truffles.

But since I do not like the nuts
I am glad someone is picking them
and enjoying the insecticide-free feast.

Lame Deer

Snacking, playing cooperative Scrabble
in an enclosed outdoor room
among artificial sunflowers,
we did not notice, at first,
a deer with an injured back leg
hobble into the backyard
on the other side of the windowpane.

The doe wanted to pass through our yard
to grass-might-be-greener neighbors'
but they were outside gardening
and shooed her away
from the other side of bushes
which separate our yards.

Having to backtrack
when her leg was injured,
setback her journey
from paved street
to our lawn, which she nibbled.
Perhaps the burgeoning blueberries
and later downfall apples will feed her.

A rotted wooden fence
has not been replaced between
our two yards, so no detours
unless someone is on security
or surveillance duty to direct
deer traffic to another yard
down the un-cushioned street.

The house on the west is fenced
for caged, howling dogs.
The deer must sense their captivity
and upgrade her solitary, safety.
Like hobos, deer must mark our house
as one of benign neglect
respite from asphalt,
resting spot to picnic.

Before the end of our game—
of tiles like mini-pavers—
she moved on, grass-refreshed.
but still limping toward hard road.

Three Deer in Our Back Yard

As subdivisions pave their habitat
more deer rest and nibble in our backyard.
One frequent visitor had viral warts,
ugly black leathery mounds.

But these three deer looked healthy,
Two bucks casually grazed near fences.
One doe under the bird-picked cherry tree
rested vigilantly.

I adjusted to turning over the cherries
to high fliers. I do not mind sharing fruit
with deer, but the fleas, ticks and excrement—
not so much.

Neighboring cats leave their dregs
and occasionally dogs
leave their calling cards,
not willing to do business in their yards.

My husband spotted the deer
during a lull in painting fascia boards.
From the window I watch
as he tries to return to his work.

He grabs a white plastic bucket
and a wooden spoon and drums,.
startling the deer to depart
toward the suburban street.

I love to witness the deer
but our son's seven-year struggle
with Lyme Disease makes me leery
of contact with wild creatures and pets.

Fencing

The neighbors built a wooden fence
like teeth to keep deer from gnawing
in their garden, birds still visit, hence
from telephone lines and branches cawing.
Deer will not spill over from our yard.
Birds treat fences with disregard.

Like teeth to keep deer from gnawing,
the fence will contain deer to feast here.
We will view the deer dining and pawing
leaving their residues as crops disappear.
We will become a pee and poop plot
which dogs and cats also use a lot.

In their garden birds still visit, hence
their produce is not totally secure.
Left to birds, squirrels, in recompense
for raccoons and nutria to procure.
We'll get aerial and grounded creatures.
Organic, pesticide-free food our features.

From telephone lines and branches cawing
Stellar jays will steal our top-limb cherries.
Squirrels indulge in hazelnut-chawing.
Deer will nibble apples and our blueberries.
Noise, net, deterrents have not stopped
any feeders. We've been topped.

Deer will not spill over from our yard.
This unweathered fence stands firm.
They have dealt an unbeatable card,
enough to make deer-dealers squirm.
Sleek strolling deers, filled with grace
have free-run of our fruitful place.

Birds treat fences with disregard.
We can peer over for fair weather chat
as the fence remains to guard
this boundary. We can live with that.
Walls and fences tend to separate
us from what we don't appreciate.

The Gourmet Tourists

Two deer stroll down our street to our backyards
to partake in the neighborhood buffet garden tour.
sampling blueberries and branch discards
until my husband strongly suggests a detour.
The deer are eating his cherished fruit
so he is shooing them in earnest pursuit.

To partake in the neighborhood buffet garden tour
requires deer taste many fruity tidbits.
When they excrete, human's mood turns sour.
Deer's stealing sends some folks into orbits.
After gardeners nourish their plentiful plantings
they view their losses with boisterous rantings.

Sampling blueberries and branch discards
all pesticide-free, organic and cherished,
when birds and deer nibble, strong words
toward creatures in whose bellies, fruit perished.
Soon it will be apples and hazelnuts
that disappear in their gluttonous guts.

Until my husband strongly suggests a detour,
flailing fists and shouting protectively,
the ravenous deer relish and rest, after they devour
fleshy repast and grass selectively.
He chases them from neighbors' yard as well
as they are unwanted, shunned clientele.

The deer are eating his cherished fruit
so he decides to create a fake fence,
dangling sun-shiny CDs along side path to re-route
entry to our prolific produce, so hence
when they return a few hours later
he's snappier than an alligator.

So he's shooing them in earnest pursuit
whenever he gets glimpses of deer.
He's given birds top limbs in cherry dispute,
as well as most hazelnuts. It's clear
deer can share downfall apples, but when
is our copious café open for us again?

Summer Storm

Light streaks across ponderous night
past gloaming glints near midnight.
Lightning is rare in Oregon
so at first I thought the TV
was somehow shooting reflective rays
into the darkness. Maybe flares.

Then light bursts like fireworks
before sky fabric rips strings of jagged threads.
Blood red crescent moon peek-a-boos black clouds.
Rumbles get louder than trains
then booms before globs or rain
pummel the ground.

Inside the flashes seem safely away,
but I recall an incident in Saipan
where a woman was struck
through a window, but survived.
At least I could close the windows
to prevent rain pouring in. Hope it's enough.

I sit out scary storm watching
late night comedic satires
to divert concern about tensions
personal and all around the world .
Comic relief sometimes works–or not.
TV could blow and lose power.

Screen darkles as I head for bed.
All is energy and mine is spent.
Mind fires locally enclosed in heavy heat.
I try a small fan   Under a sheet
I breathe deeply to sleep.
Storms will be somewhere in the morning.

Red Morning Moon

Red moon this morning
smudged by smoky haze.
In the mountains fires burn
forests, homes for days.

In the valley we hope for sun
but not blazingly hot,
after recent storm stirred fears
and left us a troubled spot.

We're jarred after jagged lightning
now striking other places
ripped through thunder toward earth
left us with rimpled faces.

Sitting here gazing out window
shadows creep toward gloaming.
Heated darkness looms elsewhere.
Thoughts toward night moon roaming.

Seasoning

My hands know to be open
and not to fist.
Gripping handlebars, hands provide
balance and direction.
I prefer to walk to see rhodies
up close as they bloom,
deceived by warming winter.
A leaden grandma in heavy shoes
slapping pavement, cold penetrating soles.

One of my grandma's hair turned snow-white,
the other's turned gull-gray as rain clouds.
We called one Mom because
our mother did.
We called the other Kitty Grandma
after her cuddled cats, but she thought
we meant Kiddie Grandma.

One grandma could cook
and the other could not.
Both Swedes drank coffee,
used the grounds to compost gardens.
The good cook baked coffee breads
and tasty Swedish fare.
The poor cook could crack our teeth
with burnt meatballs, bony fish and cardboard crusts.
Late at night I recall our diverse family dinners
at both grandmas. One soft. One hard.

Today sun soothes from blue skies
in a foggy, soggy climate,
Rays stir spirits like lightning strikes
to souls. On warmer days I watch
Stellar jays jump on abundant branches,
snitch, peck and drop cherries
out of our arm's reach. I've learned
not to raise my fist and curse these thieves,

but to share and remove snares
of nets, shiny tins, loud sounds.
We gather low-limbed, cherished cherries
and leave the unobtainable
and grounded, wounded fleshy bits
for other hungry seekers.
My palms stain red as blood
as I go inside to knead pie crust.

Yolo
You Only Live Once

I am seeking clarification
as to a final destination
and need edification
about living this incarnation.

Do we really yolo—
travel earthly lives solo
or galloping galactic Marco Polo
on a one-trick pony? Oh no!

Are we some cosmic clone
traipsing the cosmos alone
in dimensions unknown,
on planets gaseous or stone?

According to some polls
we do recycle souls
trying different roles
avoiding a black hole.

You only life once–this time
in this body, in this clime.
Prepare for change sometime
we may live time, aftertime.

Think of a role reversal
without a planned rehearsal
the stage may be universal
and the play run- eternal.

Perhaps they're diverse gene pools
places with very different rules
using more high-tech tools
learning from better schools.

All this is speculation
but requires some contemplation
lifetimes without cessation
without knowledge of creation.

I hope I grasp some insight
to traverse dark with some light
regardless of my mysterious plight
see starry beacons in the night.

Throughout the multiverse it's known
life chances are so diverse. I'm prone
to believe Earth is not alone
having sentience. E.T. phone.

***

Evening of day "Yolo" poem had begun
we're eating out and nearly done,
a guest pointed at a Mustang in fading sun
the license plate said YOLO 1.

Isolato

a person who is spiritually isolated from or out of sympathy with his or her times or society.   Dictionary.com

What sensible crone would go into her backyard
to meditate on the cloud of unknowing,
drape her mother's red cape over stooping shoulders,
sit in a collapsible blue camp chair
wear SAS shoes with Velcro flaps,
and think she'll be able to draw Gaia's chi
through her heavy shoes with sluggish lymph
to energize her ailing body and spirit—
especially when she knows she gets distracted
when trying to be contemplative.

The only sensible part is at least
I stay inside to brood when it's cold and rainy.
I am P.C. about the environment and global warming,
but I am no tree-hugger. Backyard bark is rough.
My arthritic knees do not permit hikes in forest.
My nature vision comes from cameras and eyesight.

I prefer to ponder the mysteries of life alone,
explore all media to create insight and questions,
impatient for some answers, curious what I'll find.
You would think I would know my way around
this wayward world steadfastly by now.
I dream alternatives.
Too rebellious for the religious route.
Too skeptical for the New Age
Too free-thinking to adopt another's philosophy.
Too math-phobic for scientific solutions.

Not a God groupie in publicly worshiping congregations
following strict dogma, prescribed rules and roles,
attached to often ancient hierarchies.
Bone-on-bone knees prevent kneeling.
If I were to prostrate I'd never get up.
I remain unaffiliated with organized faith.
So I will become an isolato.
I am loosely attached to this planet,
open to otherworldly options.

But I must be in the present for right now.
Perhaps it would be better to try
prayer rather than meditation.
Apparently Pagans pray outside.
But if I closed my eyes I might miss seeing something.
A writer needs to pay attention.
Who would I pray to? Angels? Guides? Cosmic Couriers?
What Prime Source or Force, Creator, God or ALL
would they report to? We are not sure what universal plan exists
and who else is out there picking up transmissions.
At night I can send my messages undercover into the dark multiverse.
A wing and a prayer could reach someone.

My backyard is like an island amid a teeming planet.
In a violent, chaotic world I seek peace.
In an inequitable nation I favor equality.
In an unjust culture I advocate justice
In my needy, beautiful community I support service and arts.
In hateful and intolerant relationships I want compassion and love.

My pinball machine brain ricochets angles.
Thought-balls bonk lights, illuminate lightbulb moments.
Certain ideas enlighten my game. My surface slants.

As I sit starry-eyed under bluing sky
on my soul island, I count on creativity
to express my discoveries— not perceived knowledge..
You would think by my seventies, my wanderlust
would have found a high way for my spiritual path
but I continue to take the dirt road less traveled.
Grateful for choice, I own my difference.

Dust to Dust

Stardust sparkles quarks to life.
House dust darkles surfaces.
Road dust blurs the view.
Gift-drift from the cosmos
can animate the inanimate
or mute earthly surfaces
with microscopic layering,
but if you can't move,
dust just cloaks.

Do I seek uncovering?
Should I swipe away dust-dull
for dust-shine?
Try feather-dust duty
for illumination, texture, color
or imagine dust motes
re-settling after aerial transport,
then ask if dusting
is worth my best use of time
or if dust's palimpsest
is my preferred way
of knowing and seeing?

Dirt Dreams

Under the pavement dirt dreams of grass.   Wendall Berry

Under the pavement flattened dirt
deprived of rain and snow
cannot see sky, but hears rumblings.

Barren asphalt and cracking concrete
writhe across the landscape
wrestle earth for wheels, divert moisture.

Dormant dirt beneath roads
can come back to life.
Farmland reverts to forest or meadow.

In desert's vast arid places
dirt gazes upon drying sun
hugs tenacious roots, dreams clouds.

Sand waves dunes,
skitters across the strand,
wind-drifters like kites, plays.

In watery areas beyond sidewalks
roadside borders bloom.
Green freely rises. Dirt quenches thirst...

Fire blackens earth, parches.
Under lava flows dirt yearns to breathe.
Soil smothers fire.

Pebbles and rocks roll and groove.
Monuments stick around. Dig in.
Dirt weathers climate change.

Stepped upon, waste disposal site, chemical dump,
mined, dirt shifts at the will of nature
and many creatures. Dirt desires lightening.

Hunkering under houses, supporting structures
dirt carries heavy weight. Life moves above.
Dirt sustains wriggling or withering roots.

Dirt nourishes and shelters. Worms,
bugs, burrowing creatures tunnel air, tickle.
Dirt seeks sun, would like to be tan.

Passageways slither in front of our home
Lawn and planting pruned and picked.
Dirt holds and hides dirty wet dreams.

Dreaming

After a conference in Austria
I decide to visit Swedish relatives.
One couple would be released
from a mental hospital
the day after I left.
Another relative is at a retirement party
from teaching and serves
an undercooked turkey.

Somewhere I teach sixth grade
in a huge, new school with no textbooks.
I decide I can wing-it awhile teaching
creative writing and choose fiction
the hero's journey stories.
But I need a math book. Other teachers
say go to the principal. On my way
my deceased mother-in-law says
I am walking better . Arm in arm
we walk to the principal's office.

A poet friend's husband confronts her
in a store for prostituting for booze.
He said she could find her own way home.
She is drunk and a party is underway.
I counsel her and other party-goers
about dealing with their drinking.

In the adjoining room a sculpture mountain.
I climb a craggy side. The top has a polished pillar
which I topple. I slide down the smooth other side.
I look back at the crumpled column and wonder
if they will know who knocked it over.

Asleep my senses do not create these images.
Am I in another parallel world?
Who creates my sentience awake or asleep?
Perhaps Shakespeare was partly right
when he said we were players on a stage
but who writes the scripts
or in a puppet show who pulls the strings?

On World Tarot Day

Tarot is a way to meditate about your life...a mirror of where you are.
Sometimes we can't see ourselves clearly without a mirror.

Teresa Pridemore

Today is World Tarot Day says
the newspaper article I carry
into the backyard with my chair and notebook.

Perhaps I am going about meditating all wrong.
I can't slurp Gaia's chi through my shoes
on patio pavers or grass.

Gaining insight through meditation
with my scattered brain might not work.
Perhaps I should shuffle some cards.

My red cape could have a more magical
or mystical purpose as I sit in potential sun
on an overcast, chilly spring day musing.

Tarot cards are tools for self-reflection and insight.
over 500 years old with a full deck of 78 cards.
They have digital divination on-line now.

Taking Tarot from a tactile experience
to a digital one is challenging. The querent
is not beside the reader. I'd choose cards.

A reading is a "momentary map" that shows
where someone is and where one might be bound.
unless free will changes direction.

Cards can help with the big picture
but we make our own choices.
Tarot is not a fortune telling tool.

I go inside and raid my stash of cards and runes
crammed in a cabinet from my New Age era
They dealt with my deep grief.

Goddess Knowledge cards from multi-cultural mythologies
allow clearer vision of our strengths, link to collective
consciousness with a worldwide pantheon of goddesses.

Heart and Soul cards by psychic Sylvia Brown
covered a variety of topics to warm heart and soul
and give insight into true meaning of life.

Sacred Path cards: discovery of self with Jamie Sams using
the strength and beauty of Native American spiritual tradition,
wisdom of sacred teachings to show ways to transform lives.

Inner Child Cards by Isha and Mark Lerner use fairy tales,
myth and nature to reawaken the child in us with archetypes
of the inner world for revelations for our journey of self-discovery.

The Fairies Oracle with Brian Froud and Jessica Macbeth:
enchanting cards to find insight, wisdom and joy, illuminate.
future, heal heart and soul with sylphs, pans, gnomes, fairies.

These boxed cards remained mostly unopened but
the signed book accompanying runes by Ralph H. Blum
was used. " a mirror for the magic of our Knowing Selves."

Tarot would take some study. Teresa Pridemore of Portland
created her deck using local symbols for interpretations.
If I did this, I would include rainbows, fairies, angels, dark chocolate.

Tarot cards are interpreted and it takes practice and knowledge.
Some say it is a dark art and some say a free-will based medium.
But like most cards it can be a vehicle for self-insight.

Cards are always somewhat of a gamble and runes a craps shoot.
But I like the feel of runes. I draw Mannaz: the Self: the starting point.
"Only clarity, willingness to change is effective now."

Be in the world, but not of it. Be not judging, narrow or closed.
Strive to live the ordinary life in a nonordinary way. A time
of major growth and rectification. Be devoted, modest and moderate.

Remember what is coming to be and passing away.
Focus on what abides and on results. Experience a true present.
Balance the self."Nothing in excess "and "Know thyself" from Delphi.

If I take this advice I'd find true direction for my life. The Poetic Edda says:
From a word to a word /I was led to a word, /from a deed to another deed,
Maybe I should cast a few more rune stones...or try free-writing.

I Punched a Rabbi

Looking at the attendees list
for our 55th high school reunion.
I spotted Michael's name
and beside it—Rabbi.
Organizers say games will
make it possible to talk
to everyone there.
What should I say to Michael?

Flashback about 57 years
to Mr Poitier's English class.
Michael sat behind me
and gleefully kicked my heels
knocking off my loafers.
For weeks in my well-behaved,
pre-Women's Lib cool,
I gently asked Michael to stop.
Apparently he did not understand no.

One frustrating day I rose my
full 5 foot two, one hundred pounds
from my chair. I faced Michael
punched him in the jaw
making him fall backwards in his chair
and sprawl on the floor
looking at me in shock.

The teacher looked at us and said,
"The little ones pack a punch
don't they, Michael" and continued
on with his Silas Marner lecture.
Today I would have been expelled.
But then I felt powerful. Michael never
played footsies with me again.

Most likely Michael has forgotten
being humiliated by a scrawny girl
or as part of his spiritual path
has forgiven me and his adolescent behavior.
But what should I say to him?
Does it matter because he is a rabbi?
What would I say to anyone I punched out?

In late-50's suburban Connecticut
after-school interaction between
Catholic, Protestant or Jewish youth
was not encouraged, inter-dating
frowned upon. Some of these highly
talented Jewish students were
children of holocaust parents, still
facing Jew Quotas at colleges.

At progressive reunions, some
of the cliques reunited and classmates
delighted getting to know one another
sometimes for the first time.
So what will I say to Michael?
I will wait to see it he mentions it.
Perhaps forgetfulness has encroached.
But if he mentions it? I need to think
what I will say to Michael?

In the News Today

In Utah bald eagles lie listless on the ground.
Many have seizures and paralysis.
Perhaps they have eaten eared grebes
infected with avian cholera.
Downed and sick eagles cannot be saved.
Scientists are baffled by mysterious disease.
Our national bird recently removed
from endangered species list,
may have to be put back on.

Along the west coast the starfish are wasting away,
losing limbs and turning into white goo.
Scientists don't know what is causing the disintegration—
bacteria, toxins, water discharge, ocean acidification?
Some suspect Japanese tsunami trash or radiation.
When the water warms, sea stars die off.
Oregon's orange and purple pisaster, five-armed starfish
may also be in danger. Broad outbreaks
make recovery more risky.

Daily we witness ailing species.
Biological diversity waning. Violent upheavals.
People cause much of this distress
for other species as well as ourselves.
Russian terrorist attacks threaten Olympics.
al-Qaida leaves a paper trail of transactions.
US credit cards can't get chips
instead of magnetic strips to protect assets.
Newspaper columns stack heavy news.

Roll On Columbia

Uncovered trains blow coal into the Columbia.
Neighbors receive "chemical trespass."
Between rocks fistfuls of crumbly, coal-black pebbles
and dust rest in protected scenic area.
All to fuel a coal-fired plant in Centralia
and export terminals in British Columbia
to ship to Asia which sends air pollution
back to Oregon on prevailing winds.

Coal from Montana and Wyoming
heads west in a quest for more
power plants and terminals.
They load the trains with "bread loaf" shape
which supposedly reduces dust.
Some spray the tops of coal cars
with sticky surfactants to limit dust.
Coal customers protest the protective tariffs.

Yet coal collects near the tracks
in river bends, where gorge gusts blow.
Water organisms face smothering
and clogged respiration.
With dark cells of Hanford leaking
near the Columbia, we might soon be saying,
"Water, water everywhere
and not a drop to drink."

Robot For President

Someday when scientists
create robots more intelligent
than humans or hybrids,
robots might want equal rights
or dominance. Someday
a robot might run for president.

Robots with no need for bio-feed or greed,
with emotions carefully calibrated,
altruistic goals, democratic leanings
might make an excellent president.
Perhaps some human frailties
would not enter the equation.

Humans would not be the head honchos,
perhaps they have lost their evolutionary edge.
If we have not treated robots well.
they might take their revenge
and treat us like second class citizens.
All our wars, protests and squabbles subdued.

Maybe we would not have created them at all
but they are E.T. controlled
and not self-controlled.
Perhaps there would be no presidency
but a dictatorship by the winning species
and they have learned to duplicate themselves.

Resources and energy required for their survival
compete with human creations.
Trust, belief, faith, freedom still elusive
unless a smart compassionate robot emerges
when human capacities have run their course.
I can only hope in the future all species are kind.

50th Anniversary of JFK Assassination
November 22, 2013

A cold sunny day.
Media frenzy of remembrance.
Tributes at the eternal flame.

Where were you when JFK was shot?
reverberates over the years.
9/11 trauma does as well.

When war and evil acts
wound a nation,
how does it heal?

Flawed JFK
not royalty or in Camelot
tried to move the nation forward.

First Catholic president like
Obama as first part Black President
they changed boundaries.

When the light of hope
diminishes, teary-eyed
we face darkness.

We are all connected to ALL,
stardust descendants
just struggling to shine.

Protesting in Comfort
Move On Vigil Against Attack on Syria
September 9th, 2013 Corvallis, Oregon

Protesters cluster on the four corners
of Van Buren and Third Streets near
two fast food places, a tire store and gas station.

The sky is clear, short-sleeve weather.
At seven traffic is brisk. Drivers honk
wave, shout out their support.

Protesters stand with signs and candles.
Walkers, wheelchairs and folding chairs
provide comfort during a trying time.

Pedestrians and bikers pass-by,
thank us for our time and commitment
to peace—this time in Syria.

Protesters of all ages, vigil veterans
and young children talk hopefully of proposed
peaceful diplomatic options in the news.

Journalists with video cameras take images
and invite comments to be sent to our Congressmen.
Like many Americans, Oregonians protest an attack.

Sitting in a camp chair, holding a white candle
wrapped in foil in a styrofoam cup given to me
by a stranger, I meet and greet in flickering light.

In my tie-dye cap, She Who Watches petroglyph shirt,
I catch-up on local and domestic news as well.
as watch fluttering hand-waves and placards.

Hand-made signs made quickly on short notice,
peace signs from other rallies held high,
swaying and stalked solid on the sidewalk.

As traffic wanes, streetlight and candlelight
make reading peace signs difficult.
Protesters begin to leave quietly.

As darkness gathers
a golden sliver of moon
bodes good wishes.

For the love of Pete

My job is to show folks there's a lot of good music in this world, and used right it may help save the planet.   Pete Seeger

Pete Seeger used music for social justice and environmental causes.
He performed his musical talents for positive change.
As I listen to our grandchildren's rap music with violent messages,
sexual innuendos and trashy language,
I do not think it will bring about the planetary reform.
Pete Seeger had in mind.

Grubby grinders, boob-baring starlets draw attention
to themselves not the ailing globe. Often
they are immersed in substance abuse,
as their talent declines. Some are suicides.
How many positive songs do they bring to the planet?
Mostly they mire in love-gone-wrong, lonely lyrics.
We are one. Outreach for Earth's survival!
How about a folk song revival? I miss folk songs
and now Pete Seeger is dead.

Remembering World War 1
        Started August 5, 1914

One hundred years ago
The world just lost its mind.
The cost we will never know
as leaders and followers all blind.
They did not really think ahead
to the horrific toll of the dead.

The world just lost its mind
The conflict went global.
What rallying call did they find
to make soldiers feel so noble,
they would sacrifice lives on the field
for little gains and would not yield.

The cost we will never know
not in machines, money or souls.
Statistics, what they pay and owe
no balance sheet for the tolls
on individuals and nations.
So many condemnations.

As leaders and followers all blind
go tally-ho into battle.,
what were the values that bind?
What realities do they rattle?
What impulses lead them to fight?
Did they improve their plight?

They did not really think ahead
and set in motion World War 2.
Hadn't enough people bled?
Did the countries start anew?
They held onto old grudges.
True intent, history fudges.

To the horrific toll of the dead,
don't we need to think peace,
listen to the many who pled
to let the warfare decrease.
We still invade, plunder, burn.
Too many people never learn.

The Red Line

Red lines can be drawn
with blood in sand.
Red lines can be metaphorical
can be re-interpreted
and erased.

Red lines can be spoken
or written on a page.
But to create red lines
threatening boundaries
requires reconsideration of options.

Red lines by leaders
against world rules
not taking account
people on both sides
of the issue are wrong.

Red lines of rhetoric
can bring war
spread beyond one country
and infect globally
bring lines of blood.

Red lines are not straight.
Too many directional shifts.
Too many blots
Too many errors
that effect us all.

Friday the 13th

Do I dare to drive today?
Accident on the way?

Will I drown in the pool?
They'll think I'm acting April Fool?

Hard candy might break a tooth?
No cell or telephone booth?

Will the computer decide to crash?
Will a friend find another to trash?

Will I say something foolish
to someone sick who looks ghoulish?

Will I confront a stranger
who could put me in danger?

Will I become paranoid
with everything I should avoid?

I'll risk dark chocolate made abroad.
Watch my funds to reduce fraud.

I won't share numbers I shouldn't
or attempt feats I know I couldn't.

I can't let superstition make me fear,
but lots of hard things happened this year.

What makes me think I'm exempt
and I'll succeed at every attempt?

Friday the 13th on Poetry month–oh!
I have daily poems many to go!

This poem will lack content and form.
Will irregularities be the norm?

But poetry and Scrabble are highlights today.
What will I do if I can't word-play?

What if I wake up and feel like crap
and don't feel better after a nap?

Since I face so much dread,
I think I'll just stay in bed.

Dam Dog Doggerel

Friends and their dog will come to visit us.
I am not a dog owner or fan.
I fear the fleas, slop and ruckus.
How am I going to adjust to this plan?
Jumpy, slobbery dogs make me annoyed.
This is a creature I've not enjoyed.

I am not a dog owner or fan.
My house is no longer even child proof.
Grandchildren are grown. I can
not be a host and be aloof.
My collections sprawl on floor and wall.
Not a safe doggy place overall.

I fear the fleas, slop and ruckus—
the need for walking and droppings on lawn.
The feeding, the petting, all the fuss
beginning near the break of dawn.
This is their child and must be inside
in their hands' reach if not beside.

How am I going to adjust to this plan
with this dog with us and in guest room?
My husband does not think we should ban
the dog to garage, but give our best room.
I don't like dogs at owner's beck and heel.
I don't like an indentured dog's life deal.

Jumpy, slobbery dogs make me annoyed
or even when they lounge about.
As companions they are employed
and for others a comfort no doubt.
But for me, they just make a mess
and I don't want dog's neediness.

This is a creature I've not enjoyed.
I prefer an independent cat.
I don't want knickknacks destroyed.
No pets. I am done with that.
Abstractly I love all creatures on Earth,
but not personally to share my berth.

Dam Dog Doggerel 2

We are running a Hound Hilton hotel.
Dealing with our guests' doggie duties,
dog's messy issues and strong smell.
Dog might have worms, tics or mite cooties.
I am kept hostage, cautiously vigilant.
I'll listen to her tongue-dropping pant.

Dealing with guests' doggie duties,
hoping for no skid marks on the floor.
Maybe puppies are considered cuties
but not this pampered paramour.
No poinsettia poison in our artificial plants.
I'll give her diligent dog training a chance.

Dog's messy issues and strong smell
make conversations with guests difficult.
My canine anxiety does not bode well.
I fear a tense visit is the result.
It is a stretch to consider her to guard.
Defining her domestic dog role is hard.

Dog might have worms, tics or mite cooties
camouflaged microscopically under groomed fur.
Her spindly, boney legs are not beauties
yet there is a kind of swag with her
for barking, digging, urine marking,
and other fragrances debarking.

I am kept hostage, cautiously vigilant,
fear damage to woven rugs, wooden floor,
collections or even an artificial plant.
I have closed my bedroom door.
To avoid tripping over unfamiliar mound
I'll keep my eyes on familiar ground.

I'll listen to her tongue-dropping pant.
Impatient, I just want her to leave.
I want to let loose my bitchy rant.
release what I really believe.
Not everyone views dogs as children. Please
do not inflict them. Hear my unwelcome pleas.

Dam Dog Doggerel 3

Today is my D-Day: Dog Day
Today is my H-Hour: Hound Hour.
This designated day is not doomsday.
Time to relax and empower.
Today could be a Day of Decision.
Time for an attitude revision.

Today is my H-Hour: Hound Hour
The mini-wolf is at the door.
White, brown-dotted, canine power
yippies, pounces across the floor.
Unleashed, rescued dog explores all over.
Sniffs, shakes, chews squeaky ball we discover.

This designated day is not doomsday.
Under table at crotch level, she sees me eat.
she stares at you when told to stay,
eager for pat or a handout treat.
Finally during a break in human talk
some dog lovers take her for a walk.

Time to relax and empower.
Practice being calm and neutral.
ignore dog demands and do not cower.
Let others have bag duties, act natural.
Dog decides to be a couch potato.
Better than an indoor tornado.

Today could be a Day of Decision
I notice her well-behaved manner.
Not much to earn her my derision.
But still no dog welcome banner.
I can decide not to react with fear
and tolerate her presence here.

Time for an attitude revision.
D-Day could be for debarkation day.
We have provided our best provision—.
guests and dumpster-ditched dog delay.
Part-whippet pooch brushed my leg for a pet.
but mixed-breed mutt hasn't won me yet.

Noisy Morning

Punctually about 6 a.m.
he slithers through a slurring sliding door
toward the kitchen to make his breakfast.
Silverware rattles as he opens the drawer.
The cupboard and dishes clash.

He fills a bowl with his daily rotation
of cereals mounded to display
diced seasonal fruits—
chop, chop, chop on the cutting board
until plopped on top.
Then soy milk spills,
walnuts clump,
foul-smelling yeast sprinkles,
with dollops of his homemade yogurt,
retrieved from refrigerator wheezing—
opening and closing.

Sometimes soy sausage sizzles
in the clanking pan on the stove.
Heating water hisses.
Whole wheat or multi-grain bread
rustles wrapper. Flub of butter tub
before spreading on toast.
Gurgling bubbles of hissing heat in coffee pot.
The creaky chair skirs across
cork flooring back and forth
from the metallic hutch eating area
to counter to refrigerator.
Occasionally he drops a utensil.
Dishes, forks and spoons will clink in sink
awaiting dishwasher.

As he gobbles his gourmet meal.
His slippers shuffle across the kitchen
with his annoying repetitive noises.
Occasionally there is a cough,
clearing of early riser's throat.
His allergy snuffle.
He is hard of hearing and wears
ear phones tuned to NPR.

I close the bedroom door
to muffle wakening sounds.
Today his cell phone rings.
I have listened too long to sleep.

Forgetfulness

Some days we are just too forgetful.
We forget appointments to our chagrin.
We leave articles and are regretful
feeling we've let dementia creep in.
        Perhaps we are too distracted.
        In remorse, we over-reacted.

We forget appointments to our chagrin.
I wrote down the wrong doctor time.
I spaced out when night class should begin,
continued on a project overtime.
        Usually I'm early, rarely late
        so when I goof up, it's hard to relate.

We leave articles and are regretful.
Husband leaves hats, coats nearly anywhere.
He gets busy and becomes neglectful.
He left his planner unaware
        until his backpack revealed it gone.
        He drove far to retrieve it, unfound by phone.

Feeling we've let dementia creep in
we fear memory loss, being absent-minded.
Has Alzheimer's sent a bulletin?
Are we brain dead, truth blinded?
        Why can't we think more clearly
        and remember things we hold dearly?

Perhaps we are too distracted
multi-tasking beyond our scope.
Circuits over-loaded, access retracted
We get too overwhelmed to cope.
        Forgetting names can be expected,
        but important events should be suspected.

In remorse we over-reacted.
Hubby and I vowed to be more vigilant.
We examined how we've acted
and hope to be more diligent.
        We may have problems with retention.
        Time to shape up and pay attention.

A Nudist

How wonderful to be a nudist
with no concern for fashion design,
strategic tattoos in full display,
all-over tans without a line.

Think how you could cut expenses
no high heels or clunky shoes,
no laces to trip on or to tie,
barefoot touch with callous clues.

What do you do about pockets, purses?
You don't need make-up–but credit cards?
Where do you dangle keys,
writing gear for scribbling bards?

How do you perform in sports,
ride animals, use gear?
You need cover for protection
to avoid bandaged souvenir.

Perhaps I'd reconsider
if lost some dragging weight,
toned up the saggy parts
or accepted my droopy state.

My scars, scabs and lymphomas
provide some bas relief.
Mono-chromed, mostly white-washed,
I'm victim of color thief.

Then I've tendency to feel cold.
I'd have to move some time,
stay inside with fake heat
or seek a sunny clime.

It's not vanity that keeps me dressed
or yearning to pay societal due,
but protection from the rough spots
and comfort in warming hues.

Loose Woman

I am a loose woman
in a gut-wrenching situation
as my intestinal innards
go rogue, race to exits.
Orifices blast like volcanoes.

Food does not stick around
to nourish me.
Weight melts away.
Energy drains.
Dehydration.
Blood, urine, stool tests,
abdominal ultra-sound
interpreted.

Three doctors, an intuitive,
massage and acupuncture therapists,
DNA health interpreter,
a natural healer, my research
all suggest possibilities.

Two gall stones roll around,
infections of various kinds,
certain foods,
medicinal reaction—
all kinds of mini-bits
causing havoc.
I get tidbits of information,
but not a comprehensive what
or effective treatment.

I yearn to be a solid citizen
whose nano-parts flow with consistency.
At this point I would not mind
being a little up-tight.

Shopping Accountably

My green shopping cart rolls down the aisle
accepting products I toss in
with no list:

1 roasted chicken
1 raisin and carrot salad in plastic container
75 calorie multi-grained, seed-killer bread
made by a convict
"We say **no** to bread on **drugs**."
1 butter with olive oil
7 non-fat yogurt
240 glucosamine chondroitin tablets
2 bags of steamed vegetables
3 bags of dark chocolate bites
for the writer's groups snack buffet

I forgot my fabric bags.
As I unload, I collapse two paper ones.
One bulges with a cinnamon bun.

Going Paleo

In Eastern Oregon in Paisley Cave
archeologists find sandals—very old,
trying to figure out how cave folk behave.
nearly 9,000 years ago, I've been told.
How was life in the Paleolithic?
Does not sound that terrific.

Archeologists find sandals—very old
stir Oregon novelist Jean Auel
to write *Clan of the Cave Bear*-millions sold.
She supports research as they dig with trowel.
The past is coming to light
illuminating ancestors' plight.

Trying to figure out how cave folk behave
is important as I'm on Paleo diet.
Like imprints on Lascaux, France cave
I'm starting a new blueprint to try it.
No carbs or sugar for hunter-gatherer folk.
But my love for dark chocolate is no joke.

Near 9,000 years ago, I've been told
cave folk used stone tools to process food.
If you were to survive, you must be bold.
Now processed foods, just not as good.
But I buy market-bought veggies and meat
and fruit as a sugary treat.

How was life in the Paleolific?
Not long for a fat diabetic.
Add the fact I'm arthritic
and the prospects are pathetic.
No more additives, for these old bones
as I live like cave kinfolk throwing stones.

Does not sound that terrific
to deny dark chocolate, give up gourmet
But results could be horrific
if I don't give up my lazy, easy way.
No smores around their campfire
so I must curb my dessert desire.

174

Birth by Land or Sea

Scientists found 80 new ichthyosaur
reptile fossils from early Triassic period
about 248 million years ago

East of Shanghai near Chaohu
in once an inland sea, skeletons
of embryos and their mother remained.

One ichthyosaur just about to be born,
Two embryos still in mother's belly
when a landslide buried them.

Born head first suggests
these primitive ichthyosaurs
lived on land, at the time of dinosaurs.

Later relatives birthed in sea
came out tail first, like dolphins.
which these torpedo body shapes resemble

Full grown they could be about three feet
ate worms and small sea creatures
with a long, thin snout.

If by land, or by sea determines
how old this species is, Delay of head
is ideal for water birth.

They need to swim to surface to breathe.
These land-born embryos could not get
through a landside to take in air.

Perfectly preserved, these reptiles
were caught in environmental disaster.
What habitat are we leaving descendants?

People pop out head-first unless breech..
Some mothers chose to deliver in water.
Ichthyopterygians evolved. Will we live that long?

Teeth

Doctors removed a tumor
from a baby boy's brain
with several full-grown teeth.
Doctors hope to learn to cure
diseases or grow new organs
from this discovery.

Scientists discovered DNA
in ancient dental plaque–
a fossilized microbial world,
from four skeletons found
in a medieval German convent.
More DNA is found in teeth plaque
than in damaged bone.
Mineralized teeth, a hard matrix,
a time capsule, a game changer,
microbial Pompeii for researchers.

Now dental hygienists scape our plaque,
encourage good dental health with flossing
But this ancient plaque gives details.
of diet, disease from these teeth,
provides complete genomes.
Today with so many whitened
and scrubbed teeth, future researchers
could find a blank slate
and need to dig DNA elsewhere.

All the years of brushing and cleaning
my teeth, braces to keep them straight,
efforts to keep them in my gums
and cavities at bay would confound
probers of my toothy remains.
My endeavors only of use
for my lifetime.
So why not leave cremains?

Scarlet Letters

A E S C N–
letters smudged off my keyboard,
recovered and identified
by red circle stickers.
W L and D are erasing.

Left-side dots emblazon
my most-used letters.
My favored hand touches keys.
I still look after decades of typing.
Unblemished punctuation,
numbers and commands
surround impounded letters.

The black-outs confused my fumble fingers,
my non-tech mind.
Just small white curl remnants
were clues and a few guesses
to which letters were missing.

These bright bubble letters
attract and distract me
from their white-etched companions,
Before keys all blur black,
I will buy multi-colored dots
to stick on all the keys,
so when I peek at my enhanced keyboard
I'll behold a pointillist palette.

Computer Rant

This computer will not connect
to email or Internet many times.
No matter what I select
it punishes me for my crimes.
Programs unsupported
won't do what's purported.

To email or Internet many times
this old clunker stalls, says no.
Won't let me write my rhymes
or research where I want to go.
Even when it goes into the shop
the problems just never stop.

No matter what I select
the keys do not get me there
My system doesn't protect
reminds me to beware.
Things are getting obsolete.
This desktop can't compete.

It punishes me for my crimes.
I use WordPerfect not Word.
It balks and my temper climbs.
I wish I was a high-tech nerd.
I get so very frustrated.
I need to get updated.

Programs unsupported
leave me with little choice.
My ideas can't be transported.
I will have lost my voice.
If all my files are lost.
I'll have paid a high cost.

Won't do what's purported
so I must get a laptop.
It's much better some reported.
Perhaps it's due for a swap.
I've had this flop for many years.
Perhaps it's time for happy tears.

Dolls

Are
dolls
soul-less
replicas,
inanimate things
animated by human touch?

Are
dolls
exact
images–
imaginative
interpretations of people?

Are
dolls
just toys,
collections,
objects to play with
or manipulate to our will?

Are
dolls
a thing
of beauty—
what is best in us
reflected in art or in craft?

Are
dolls
mirrors
of ourselves,
mysterious and
inscrutable—something to hold?

Are
dolls
designed
to tempt us
to elicit love,
a trial partner to learn with?

Are
dolls
silent
except when
programmed to say just
what we want to hear or to say?

Are
dolls
named right,
too vaguely
referred to, perceived,
too carelessly spoken about.

Are
dolls
truly
reflections
of people wanting
to escape the risks of breathing?

Spiritual Quest

In my quest to be more spiritual
I explore otherworldly ideas.
I examine traditional ritual.
I question several areas.
Organized religion binds the mind.
Individual spirituality is freer I find.

I explore otherworldly ideas.
Many ways to relate to the divine.
Read and watch many medias,
but not hooked by their line.
If God exists within ALL,
what entity do we call?

I examine each traditional ritual—
some admittedly bizarre.
Blood transformation seems critical
from Mayan blood-letting to jihad war,
communion wafer and wine,
No Friday fish. Don't slaughter swine.

I question several areas.
Not raining down from cloud of unknowing
is higher wisdom—lost in seas?
Perhaps my doubt and indecision's showing.
Science and spirituality can they mesh,
bring connection of cosmos, mind and flesh?

Organized religion binds the mind.
Tight gender roles demean women.
Few power roles, often left behind.
Mutilated genitals destroys hymen.
Male hierarchy sometimes a pedophile.
Cults dominate choice.   Meanwhile

individual spirituality is freer I find.
Search for meaning, service and love
is difficult in Earth School, often unkind.
Seeking comfort and guidance from above
when we should be looking within
not through robotic religions but angelic kin.

Puzzled Omniverse Ort

Spiritual pundits ponder cosmic light.
Supposedly I am an infinitesimally small
bit in the Creator's soup that sustains
us, all-in-one in the same container.
Each of us a God-ort. I am in a serving
of the Earth reality...currently...apparently.

Spiritual pundits indicate our purpose
as dipping into the "spiritual jar."
to cash in on Akash knowledge
which helps us rise our consciousness
and vibration to share the gifts.
we can bring to better the planet.

Spiritual pundits meditate trying
to find some enlightenment
as to universal laws and their processes
on this planet. I am supposed to piece
the light puzzles to increase energy
for this Earth energy test
which passes the results
to the fabric of time and existence
to the Great Central Sun.

Spiritual pundits dismiss karma as passe
but not reincarnation. They talk of spiritual truth
which resides within each of us,
even if not evident or expressed. They speak of quantum
akashic inheritance, galactic ancestor knowledge, Three Winds,
breaching spiritual contracts for a chance
on a more user-friendly planet, but they contend
life contracts are in invisible ink and re-writeable.
We should explore spiritual logic and lots of love

Spiritual pundits share their wisdom
and promise the planet is going through
areas of quantum discovery with new tools.
Seems vibes are rising and civilizations
will get transformed. New energy will awaken
our intuitive potentials to remember truths.
We are in a spiritual relay race where some
of us get to the finish line faster.

Instead of meditating in the backyard,
blocking Gaia's chi with rubber soles,
channeling distractions, perhaps I should be
reading and thinking more for understanding.
There is a lot for a winded omniversal ort to absorb
beside the benefits of sunshine..

With my arthritic knees I can"t run hurdles
and even participate in a relay.
No spiritual track star, my soul's journey
with assisted steps,
will be the pacing of my spiritual curiosity
which will prepare me
for the Wind of Transition
with hope at my back.

Little Things

The soul is the lure of our becoming. Jean Houston

a skosh of joy
an ort of sustenance
during a time of turbulence.

tiny bits of hope
when it's cold and foggy
when chaos stalks clarity

expression stunted
impact thwarted
small steps forward

thoughts compressed
compacted to explode
with volcanic ashy words

microscopic surveillance
micro becomes macro
explodes quarks of discontent

under-sized solutions
to over-sized problems
little things can gnaw

tiny acts become larger
create change
and connection

remember infinitesimal
in a conscious cosmos
among all the sparks of ALL

Ode to My Red Cape

My mother's plain, red cape hooks and droops
on a Shaker peg in the hallway
like the witch's red cape on coat rack
in local production of Bell, Book and Candle.
Often it is tossed carelessly, crumples in a chair
waits for me to unravel folds
and take it outside.

My mother wore the cape to cloak skirts
above her tan, knee-high leather boots.
I wear this cape over strident pants
with black leather SAS shoes.

This cape clutches neck with Velcro–
a loose noose or lasso
with an extension tail-scarf that flips
over the left shoulder. No neck tie.
Cut umbilical cord to buttons
ripcord to zippers.

I fling flap so not tight enough to choke
or strangle like Isadora Duncan's scarf,
but secure enough to buffet fierce winds.
Let it writhe in air,
avoid getting entangled, snagged or caught.
It curls around my neck like a cat's tail,
does not coil like a snake.

My red cape undulates over arms
and over back like waves,
flaps at fire, fans then douses flames,
billows to music and muses,
bellows to breath–
my magical cape for song and celebration.
I move undercover for escapades of excitement.
A cape is impractical near machine.

My red cape does not usually enclose my head in a hood,
like Red Riding Hood fleeing wolf or rich-robbing Robin Hood,
hooded beggar, penitent, haunted hoodlum,
teen's hoodie, ornamental ruffle on academic gown,
cloistered nun's wimple, sheltering hijab
jurist's robe or ardent prayer shawl,
mantilla, bridal veil, head scarf or capapie.
My red cape is not dangerous
bullfighter's cape enraging bulls,
Dracula's cover for his lust for blood
or Devil's red hot search for souls.

My red cape drapes like curtains to open musing,
not my grandmother's fox clenched over her gentle shoulders.
No granny shawl, medieval chaperon. Pilgrim's cloak,
clerical ferraiolo, liturgical vestment,
vampire cover-up, royal robe, capelet,
actor's costume in historical dramas,
flamboyant male cloaks
flaunting Lord Byron and Oscar Wilde,
masterful back canvases
for Salvador Dali and Leonardo da Vinci.
For heroic Harry Potter, arm concealer for Emperor Napoleon,
Liberace's rhythmic robes, Red Baron Snoopy.
Evoke red phantom of Anne Sexton, caped syllabic Marianne Moore,
Disney's sleepy Snow White. Cinderella racing from the ball.

My red cape is no delicate, crocheted cape
or luxuriously velvet, alpaca, satin or silk–
more like my mother-knit, fringed white poncho,
a red flag of an aging Hippie.

Not big enough for sleeping bag,
When smoothed it can be a blanket in car,
snuggle on couch, comforter on plane.

Secretly I don't want to tamp wild flappings in wind.
Sometimes a cape just makes me feel "cool".
Is a cape a blatant bid for attention or power?

A cape to es-cape lands-cape
to cape jutting into my uncharted waters,
capsule to cosmos.

My capeskin of fleece
my scarf-skin overlay
is simple, not embroidered.
My red cape is metamorphic, metaphoric.

My red cape is a wrapper
botched mummy job bleeding through bandages
red licorice twist, dark chocolate Dove foil,
rolled rug, crystal ball cover.
Healing iron lung helping me breathe,
prayer wheel unable to spin,
a turtle shell when I stick my neck out,
red repair patch for a gigantic quilt square,
shield from reality, rocket to fantasy.
No claustrophobic MRI bullet
I will never enter again.
Only muse-ful excursions booked.

When seated my red cape covers,
warms my cranky knees
hugs me snug, keeps me under wraps.
My wrapped cape is
Valentine heart, ripe strawberry
sheathed sword, hot tomato,
cherry jelly roll, stuffed wrapped turkey sandwich,
burrito with spicy sauce, red jelly bean,
scarlet tulip bud about to blossom.

When standing my red cape wings
cardinal ready for flight,
order of angels with colored wingspans
or a bleeding Earth angel.
I do not conjure
grim, grey-winged fallen angels
or rigid plane wings.

My red cape is magical
like a magician, witch, wizard,
Wonder Woman, Superman,
seeress, Nostradamus–
flares like a fashion model's designer cape
down runway.

Red light,
stop sign to a shroud.

Swish a wish for a dancing cape.
Martha Graham's shroud breaking free to move.
Loie Fuller's flowing gossamer veils.
Derek Hough's dazzling cape work
during paso double on Dancing with the Stars.
Beguiling belly dancers,
slashing Latin dancer's capes,
wings for indigenous bird dances

My red cape leaves arms unsheathed.
Hands fumble, reach from beneath folds.
Barrier to weather and cold,
a cape warms body and soul,
wet blanket absorbs rain
solar panel receives sun.

My red cape is a magic carpet,
ground cover for spontaneous picnic,
not a prayer rug for un-knee-ables.

A cape is mysterious as Greta Garbo,
cultured for opera,
playful prom wrapper,
elegant covering for a gala,
designed not to crush or hide gown,
explosive is a Christmas cracker
pulled at both ends.

Determinedly I march outside,
a jingle makes me giggle:
Does my cape hang low
as I wobble to and fro?
Does it tie me in a knot
or release what I forgot?
Do I flip it over my shoulder
like a Continental soldier?
Does my cape hang low?

Does my cape wind-flow
as I waiver on the go?
Does it do as I please
or free me in the breeze?
Does it warm poetic thought
or wrap wisdom I have sought?
Does my cape wind-flow?

Should I wear my light blue zippered jacket?
Mostly I wear my blue coat in public
unless it is an artsy occasion or poetry reading.
When I meditate privately in the back yard,
I prefer my red cape.
Where am I going today?
Do I risk my red cape?

Acknowledgments

Sources of these Poems:
Poems gleaned from Red Cape Capers files written 2011-2015.

Book:
Winging-It: New and Selected Poems

Chapbooks:
Red Cape Capers
April Poems 2012
April Poems 2013
Light-Headed

Other Poetry Books by Linda Varsell Smith

Cinqueries: A Cluster of Cinquos and Lanternes
Fibs and Other Truths
Black Stars on a White Sky: Selected Poems
Poems That Count
Poems that Count Too
Winging-It: New and Selected Poems

Chapbooks:
Being Cosmic
Intra-Space Chronicles
Light-Headed

On-Line Web-Site Books: @ www.rainbowcommunications.org
Syllable of Velvet
Word-Playful
Poetluck

www.ingramcontent.com/pod-product-compliance
Lightning Source LLC
LaVergne TN
LVHW011349080426
835511LV00005B/204